Paul Kofman (PhD, Erasmus University [...] Professor of Finance at the University [...] 2012, Professor Kofman became Dean o. [...] Economics. Paul's research interests and publications are in quantitative and behavioural finance and the regulation of financial markets. He was one of the founding directors of the Australian Research Council–funded Financial Integrity Research Network. With his colleague Clare Payne, Paul introduced one of the first online subjects at the University of Melbourne, 'Ethics in Finance'. With his colleague Sean Pinder, Paul also designed and developed the first Coursera MOOC specialisation, 'Essentials of Corporate Financial Analysis and Decision Making', in partnership with BNY Mellon.

Clare Payne (BA LLB, Macquarie University) specialises in the field of ethics in business. She commenced her career as an employment lawyer and then managed the Integrity Office of a global investment bank. Clare was a founding director of The Banking and Finance Oath, a not-for-profit that advocates a Hippocratic-type oath for those in finance. Clare is also a Fellow of The Ethics Centre and an Ambassador for Tobacco Free Portfolios. Clare was awarded the Inaugural Ethics in Finance Prize by the Observatoire de la Finance, Geneva; is a World Economic Forum Young Global Leader; and has been recognised by the *Australian Financial Review* and Westpac as one of their '100 Women of Influence'. As a former marathon swimmer, having swum solo around Manhattan, Clare has raised significant funds for the not-for-profit sector and continues to be actively involved in addressing a range of social issues.

A MATTER OF TRUST

OF

THE PRACTICE OF ETHICS IN FINANCE

PAUL KOFMAN & CLARE PAYNE

MELBOURNE
UNIVERSITY
PRESS

MELBOURNE UNIVERSITY PRESS
An imprint of Melbourne University Publishing Limited
Level 1, 715 Swanston Street, Carlton, Victoria 3053, Australia
mup-contact@unimelb.edu.au
www.mup.com.au

First published 2017
Text © Paul Kofman and Clare Payne, 2017
Design and typography © Melbourne University Publishing Limited, 2017

Cover design by Design by Committee
Typeset by Megan Ellis
Printed in Australia by McPherson's Printing Group

National Library of Australia Cataloguing-in-Publication entry

Kofman, Paul, author.

A matter of trust: the practice of ethics in business/Paul Kofman, Clare Payne.

9780522871708 (paperback)
9780522871715 (ebook)

Includes index.

Finance—Moral and ethical aspects.
Economics—Moral and ethical aspects.
Social responsibility of business.
Payne, Clare, author.

For those who need a little faith, or encouragement.

Long live
the book.

Clare.
2019.

CONTENTS

FOREWORD
by Dr Simon Longstaff AO

Uncomfortable as it may be for those concerned, the media's focus on unethical conduct within banking and finance underlines the importance of the industry to society (and not just the economy). The truth is that public concern about the ethics of society's bankers reflects a general understanding of a simple fact: banking really matters. For centuries, and in the face of enduring controversy about issues like usury, banks (and associated financial institutions) have been meeting basic human needs. Insurance has enabled members of the community to spread the burden of risk. Credit has allowed individuals and organisations to invest in their dreams and the prospect of a better future. Savings facilities have allowed stable stores of wealth to be held safe. In combination, financial institutions have played a vital role in enabling prosperity—not just for the few but the many.

All of this has been built on a foundation of great private and public utility combined with trust. It was (and remains) an extraordinary thing that a promissory note written in Pisa could be presented half a world away, in London, with every expectation that it would be honoured. It is extraordinary that people will entrust a banker to receive and hold the bulk of their wealth, in the certain belief that it will be returned when called for.

The whole edifice of banking and finance has been built on a surprisingly fragile foundation of confidence. That is why the scandal is so great when bankers (and their institutions) are revealed to have acted in ways that betray trust. It matters not that the perpetrators are relatively few in number. It matters not that the majority of people in the industry feel just as betrayed as the hapless victims among their customers. When the foundations of trust are undermined—even just a little—then the whole structure is rocked.

Of course, it does not help that the industry has often organised itself along lines that support (and sometimes drive) unethical behaviour. Remuneration policies, product design, a million small signals embedded in the ordinary structures of banking, have played their role in divorcing technical mastery from ethical restraint. For the most part, the adverse results have been unintended, often overseen by people of exemplary character and good will. But that is no excuse, and does not undo the great harm that offsets the considerable good to be found on the balance sheet of banking and finance.

Unfortunately, the industry (along with many others) ultimately has failed to understand that 'ethics' is vastly different to 'compliance'. The latter can be achieved in conditions of 'dumb obedience'. The former requires much more—the development and maintenance of a culture in which every participant possesses and employs a constructively critical mindset. It requires leaders who never accept the status quo simply because 'everyone does it' or because 'it has always been done this way'.

To embrace 'reflective practice' as part of what it means to *be* a banker requires both sound judgement and moral courage. This book makes the case for choosing to be that kind of banker—and how it should be given practical effect.

FOREWORD
by Greg Medcraft, Chairman, ASIC

Trust is a business asset. But building trust with customers has become far more challenging in the current environment, partly because the way in which customers interact with businesses has changed. Our commercial interactions are no longer, as they once were, with people we know directly. We now use digital technologies to transact, search for information, share our personal details—taking a leap of trust that we are safe and our best interests are accounted for. These same digital technologies allow word-of-mouth and feedback to be magnified by social media, so customers can let businesses—and the wider community—know if they have met or exceeded expectations, but they will also let them know when they have crossed the trust line. Listening to the crowd and its messages through various channels requires a degree of accountability on the part of our institutions, and on our part as professionals.

As my term as Chairman of the Australian Securities & Investments Commission comes to a close, I reflect on how this book, *A Matter of Trust*, can help us understand how to build and sustain business trust, or rebuild it once it has been lost.

Clare Payne and Paul Kofman have set out to examine trust from many angles: how a fall in trust in our financial entities has a corresponding fall in reputation, the social contract we as consumers grant these institutions, good governance principles, the duties to customers and shareholders, situations where conflicts of interest can arise and how they can be managed, possible ways forward, and how ethics can be a pathway to better practice. This multidimensional approach to examining trust reflects the complexity of doing business today. Creating a sustainable business is not only about the quality of the product or service that is delivered. It is also about the quality of an organisation's conduct, how it operates internally and represents itself externally. If the conduct of a business and its values are not aligned with customer outcomes, it is easy to see how a trust deficit will emerge, and this will impact the long-term sustainability of a business. Trust must be built through a company's brand and reputation, which is a logical result of how it treats its customers and looks after their interests.

At ASIC, we continue to encourage organisations to reflect on their culture, and how it enables or encourages the unfair treatment of investors and consumers. A sound culture, and the conduct that can stem from this culture, is fundamental to community trust and confidence.

The Banking and Finance Oath is a project facilitated by The Ethics Centre and is an industry-led initiative, designed to highlight the founding moral and ethical principles of the industry and remind individuals of their broader commitment to society now and in the future.

As a leader of my organisation, I signed The Banking and Finance Oath. The first line of the oath is 'Trust is the foundation of my profession'. And so it should be.

AUTHOR'S NOTE

I am very grateful that Paul contacted me when I was managing the Integrity Office of Macquarie Bank and invited me to deliver a guest lecture on ethics in finance for his students at the University of Melbourne. Paul then had the vision to offer a complete course on ethics in finance and we set out to design and develop it together. We believe that a course dedicated to ethics in finance provides a valuable contribution to a student's education and helps prepare them as professionals, giving them a deeper understanding of their role in upholding ethical standards and respecting the integrity of financial systems.

Writing a book is a natural development of our work and interest in ethics in finance. Australia's financial system is admired globally, and therefore a text that applies an ethical lens to the global context as well as to Australia's systems and people, is a much-needed contribution we are pleased to have made.

Of course, Paul and I don't always agree, perhaps no surprise with my background as a lawyer working in finance and Paul's as an academic and then faculty dean. Paul sometimes thinks I am far too lenient on the sector (I prefer to see myself as realistic) and at times I feel he is too extreme in drawing conclusions (he might view these as considered). But through the practice of ethics we manage to find our way, and I feel fortunate to have learned a lot from an unexpected companion.

In *A Matter of Trust* we present to you our thoughts on ethics in finance. We believe that an ethical finance sector is crucial, and that each individual has an opportunity to make a valuable contribution. We have always been in complete agreement that this is all a matter of trust.

Clare Payne, August 2017

INTRODUCTION
What's Going on?

From the marble trading floors of Wall Street to the dirt floor of a microfinance lender in rural Sumatra, finance touches everybody's lives. From small personal loans to collateralised debt obligations, it promises solutions for a better, more prosperous future. But not much in life is guaranteed, and financial outcomes may not match expectations. As financial transactions span time, they are anchored by expectations of future commitments that depend on the trust between the parties involved. When that trust is undermined, it threatens the very fabric of our financial system. While the direct consequences may only amount to customer disappointment, the financial crisis of 2007–08 highlighted how all of us may be impacted indirectly when whole economies are jeopardised by financial mismanagement.

The tax-funded bailouts of major financial institutions highlighted the intrinsic moral hazard of our global financial system. Amidst the public outcry, some commentators demanded a complete overhaul of the system: the breaking up of banks, re-regulation of markets and institutions, and abolition of recent financial innovations. Yet reality dictates that it's hard, impossible even, to wind back the financial system, its institutions and intermediaries. And would we even want to return to an imagined era of better days? After all, even the system's most ardent critics agree that financial innovation has enabled economic development and brought prosperity.[1] But does it have the ability to do better, and perhaps convince people it can do good? To answer that question, we need to address the ethics of banking and finance.

According to public perception, financial institutions have a difficult relationship with ethics. Greed, dishonesty, fraud, disloyalty and deception are just a few of the accusations undermining trust in the sector's ethical behaviour. Annual surveys of perceptions of professional integrity and ethics indicate that public trust in financial institutions has hit rock bottom. It hasn't always been like that. When these surveys were first conducted in the early 1970s, bankers were still held in high esteem. They were regarded as pillars of society. You entrusted your bank manager with your life's savings, and you could rely on that manager to honour the bank's promises to look after your money.

Of course, even in the days when banks were considered reputable institutions, there were occasional financial scandals, scams and poor advice. These unfortunate incidents were invariably attributed to rogue individuals who violated their bank's code of conduct. As these were isolated incidents, severe punishment of the individual was expected to deter others, thereby upholding the trust in, and reputation of, the institution. None of that has changed, but something else did.

Sometime during the 1980s, banks turned into financial institutions, not unlike the establishment of industrial conglomerates around the same time. Growth through mergers and acquisitions, and a need for diversification of business lines, became possible and was made necessary following a wave of global financial deregulation. This deregulation boosted competition and instantly changed banks' behaviour in protecting and gaining market share. In the global marketplace, this often involved a more aggressive stance towards gaining and generating business, and a prioritisation of shareholders' interests over other stakeholders' interests.

This change of attitude was acknowledged in 2002 by the CEO and chairman of Wells Fargo & Company, Richard Kovacevich, in a statement to shareholders:

We're pleased to say more of our customers are bringing us more of their business. That's the core of our vision—to satisfy all our customers' financial needs and help them succeed financially ... The more business customers bring us, the more time and money they save, the more loyal they are to Wells Fargo, the more interested they are in bringing us more of their business. This results in market-share growth that generates double-digit profit growth and a higher stock price.[2]

As a consequence of deregulation, the financial sector prospered and proliferated. This triggered strong demand for finance professionals, more than could be met by trained supply. Prominent financial institutions became the employer of choice for an increasingly university-educated workforce. But unlike other professions, such as accounting, the qualifications bar was never set particularly high for entry to the finance profession. Motivated by very attractive salaries, perks and performance bonuses, and the sheer excitement and glamour, some adverse workforce selection was bound to happen. That may have compromised professional competence in the sector.

Have these changes made banking less ethical? The media certainly seems to suggest so. Negative coverage of the financial sector is common: an insider trader imprisoned, an investment scheme leaving pensioners bereft, a bank manipulating interest rates. Stories abound about banks repossessing mortgaged homes during economic downturns, declaring farmers bankrupt in the middle of a drought, or encouraging credit card spending despite customers being already in arrears, suggesting a ruthless attitude and scant regard for customers' welfare. But it was only when the global economy started to be affected that populist politicians linked financial deregulation to unethical bank practices leading to systemic economic woes. As a result, bank bailouts and new regulations, including Sarbanes-Oxley, Dodd-Frank and Basel III, reset the rules of the global financial system to curtail some of its excesses.

Of course, it could just be because of our improved access to information (and social media) that only recently have these stories come to light. Not knowing about unethical behaviour does not imply its absence, and financial sector business practices may have been no more ethical in the past than they are today. But that is no excuse for current bad practice. If anything, our awareness of unethical practices should help us address the issues and where possible rectify bad behaviours.

The introduction of socially responsible investment funds that subscribe to the analysis of environmental, social and governance principles, of peer-to-peer lending platforms, crowdfunding and microfinance, are just some of the positive signs that this is happening. We could call this response 'alternative finance', and it might be tempting to think that it is, by construction, free from ethical pitfalls, as it was developed to counteract unethical traditional banking practices. Yet each of these new initiatives poses new ethical challenges.

Our hope is that by highlighting the importance of the public good of finance, and by empowering individuals through ethical practices, we can influence the sector for the better. We don't seek to apportion blame for every unethical act exposed by the media. We recognise the strong and lasting contribution to societal welfare that finance has made. But we also observe its weaknesses and the opportunity to do better. Therefore, this book provides the new and experienced finance professional with a broad overview of the key ethical issues as they occur in day-to-day financial decision-making. From changing public perceptions and expectations to the pivotal role of trust, from duties and obligations to conflicts of interest and emerging ethical challenges, this book proposes a framework to make business decisions in a morally sound and ethical way.

1

MONEY FOR NOTHING
Reputation, Trust and Ethics
Paul Kofman

Reputations, which are built over time, are a record of past performance, while trust is forward-looking. A bank's track record in delivering good, fair and reliable service helps build customer trust in its future performance. Those customers will return, and the word will spread to prospective new customers, which will enhance the bank's future prospects. A bad reputation, on the other hand, erodes trust. It makes customers think twice before entrusting a bank with their business. It reduces the likelihood of repeat business from customers who have experienced the reason for the bank's poor reputation, and new customers may be even harder to attract.

Reputation can build or break trust, and trust is the key to a successful and sustainable banking business. There is a tacit understanding in the banking sector that a loss of reputation is tantamount to the end of a career in banking. In response to his dismissal for a breach of professional conduct, former Bank of America employee Thomas Chen stated: 'We just need to re-establish our reputation because without that you can't be an investment banker'.[1]

Individuals are likely to take pride in being part of a reputable industry. The loss of that reputation can hurt morale and may affect work cultures and individual behaviours. A bad reputation may even make an individual reluctant to disclose their work or employer in conversation with friends and strangers. A 2006 Australian television commercial made this point rather poignantly. When the host of a barbecue reveals that he is a banker, a sudden silence descends on the party and people look shocked. The palpable tension is only broken when the flustered host tells everyone which bank he works for. That bank's reputation is apparently different from the 'typical' bank, so conversation resumes, and the guests smile and acknowledge the host as a 'good guy' working for a 'good bank'.

By reinforcing the message that banks in general have a bad reputation, the bank in this television ad plays a dangerous game in portraying itself as the stand-out. In addition, this is unlikely to be of great benefit when conducting business through public trust. An individual's reputation clearly needs to be supported and sustained by the sector's reputation before that individual can expect public trust and trade on it. Of course, the sector consists of organisations as well as individuals. The organisation to which an individual belongs therefore also has a bearing on the public's perception of trust. In judging a sector's reputation, the public is likely to consider the average, or typical, behaviour of its representatives, be they organisations or individuals. Unfortunately, this provides an opportunity for less scrupulous individuals to benefit from the sector's reputation and thereby discourage any investment in upholding or improving that reputation.

Safeguarding professional and industry reputations has always been challenging. To ensure that a sector's standing didn't sink to the lowest level among its representatives, medieval guilds—the predecessors of today's accreditation bodies—were established to secure the long-term reputation of certain professions (craftsmen and merchants). The merchant associations' motivations were undoubtedly protectionist by limiting and restricting professional access. Performing to exceedingly high standards became a prerequisite for aspirational apprentices to be considered for admission. And even after being admitted, a lapse in maintaining those standards could be sufficient grounds for the guild to levy fines, or even expel the miscreants. The guilds were clearly aware that a single individual's misbehaviour could lastingly dent the whole profession's reputation and thereby damage all members' business interests.

Reputation had its own rewards for the guilds and its members— business profits, promotion, status and so on—but establishing a reputation and then jealously guarding it came at a price. The guilds imposed a significant professional entry cost through lengthy apprenticeships and excruciating professional examinations. Ultimately, the economic cost of the guilds' protectionist nature, and nepotism in apprenticeships, led to their demise. Merchants opted out and, supported by innovation and economic growth, became capitalist entrepreneurs and created corporations. Apprenticeships disappeared, replaced by a labour force. The crafts could not compete and either disappeared or were absorbed into the new corporations. Responsibility for the maintenance of professional standards shifted from the individual to the institution. Entry to the profession was no longer strictly supervised, but rather was left to economic demand and competition between institutions.

The guilds' demise had much to do with the advent of capitalism and free markets, including free access to professions. Of course, the guilds were mainly restricted to the 'craft' professions. There never was a guild for a finance profession. While the guilds have disappeared, various professional accreditation agencies (such as those for actuaries and accountants) nowadays act in similar ways and attract similar criticism for making access to the professions unnecessarily restrictive, thereby diminishing competition and driving up prices. Yet, their absence in other corporate sectors, like banking and financial advice, may well contribute to consistently low levels of reputation and public trust.

IN THE PUBLIC EYE

Polls and surveys seek public opinion about a range of aspects of our lives, including the reputations of various professions and service providers. The intent of such surveys is to provide insights for the industries in question, and at times they have resulted in enhanced consumer protection—they can tell consumers to be wary and alert when dealing with certain professions or service providers that have a bad reputation. Ideally, those poorly rated will take notice and set out to improve their reputations accordingly. But disappointingly, longitudinal trust surveys reveal that relative rankings are stable, if not entirely stagnant. For example, a 2006 report entitled Treating Customers Fairly, by British consumer analyst Mintel, found that financial institutions continue to be challenged by a lack of public trust.[2]

According to the Mintel report, when British consumers were asked which groups out of twenty types of professionals would treat them fairly, they rated finance professionals particularly poorly. Pension companies were perceived as behaving fairly by just 7 per cent of those surveyed. Investment managers came out even worse, receiving only 4 per cent approval. Financial advisers were rated slightly better, considered as trustworthy by 12 per cent of those surveyed, followed by insurance companies at 10 per cent. Accountants and lawyers also appeared low on the fairness league table. Doctors, on the other hand, emerged from the survey with a rating of highly trustworthy (in relative terms)—they were the only profession that managed to win the favour of over 50 per cent of consumers.

Mintel's analysis was published precisely one year *before* the onset of the 2007–08 global financial crisis. If investment managers had an image problem at the height of the bull market, then surely after

RANKING ON ETHICS AND HONESTY

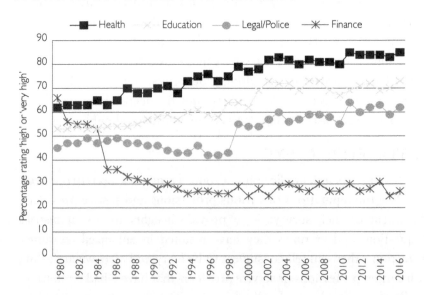

Source: Based on survey data from Roy Morgan Research, 'Roy Morgan Image of Professions Survey 2016: Nurses Still Easily Most Highly Regarded', 11 May 2016, http://www.roymorgan.com/findings/6797-image-of-professions-2016-201605110031

the stock market collapsed in the next few years, their ranking would descend further, right? Pension funds, for example, were fully funded and generated very good returns in 2006. After some customers lost entitlements, faced increased premiums, and had to postpone retirement, one would have thought those pension funds might be adversely affected in the ranking table. Well, no. There was in fact very little evidence of such adjustments by the public. That observation suggests that the actual loss of money does not drive the public perception of banks. Banks' reputations fare just as poorly in good times as in bad times.

The above graph, drawn from the results of an annual survey conducted from 1980 until 2016, illustrates the evolution of public perception of the ethical and honesty standards of four broad professions in Australia. The survey results corroborate Mintel's 2006 findings for Britain. The health profession is regarded as highly ethical and honest. Education comes a close second, followed by the legal/police area. Finance and business management, however, languish at the bottom, with only one in four surveyed subscribing to an ethical finance sector. It would be tempting to attribute some of the differences to the public preferencing public services as more trustworthy. But with increasing private provision of health (and education), that is not so clear.

Another striking feature in the above figure is the stark decline of the finance sector in the first ten years (the 1980s) of the sample. To better understand this decline, it is instructive to consider the heterogeneity of the sector. The next figure illustrates the ethics/honesty rankings for five subgroups in the finance sector, again from 1980 until 2016. The public perception of accountants, insurance brokers and stock brokers has not changed markedly over this time. The perception of bankers, however, has dropped dramatically from almost 70 per cent to just over 30 per cent, crossing below the consistent ranking of accountants. One could conclude this may be related to Australia's decade of financial deregulation.

An interesting feature of the graph is the very low ranking for brokers, around 15 per cent, which is significantly less than for financial planners. While both are segments where commissions have created significant potential for conflict of interest, financial planners seem to have benefited from a slightly better public perception. It is interesting to ponder how and why the public discriminate between these somewhat

RANKING ETHICS AND HONESTY IN FINANCE OCCUPATIONS

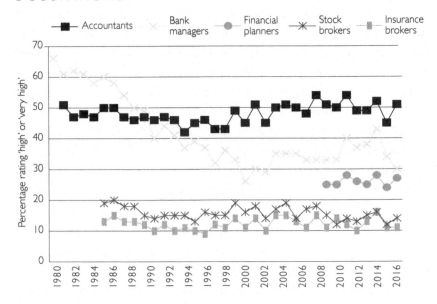

Source: Based on survey data from Roy Morgan Research, 'Roy Morgan Image of Professions Survey 2016: Nurses Still Easily Most Highly Regarded', 11 May 2016, http://www.roymorgan.com/findings/6797-image-of-professions-2016-201605110031

comparable occupations. A related factor may be that financial advice is provided in face-to-face customer relationships, whereas brokers' services are sometimes provided in a manner considered less personal.

The overriding feature of the Australian survey, and similar surveys in other countries with sophisticated financial institutions, is the consistently poor public perception of the finance sector. The Chicago Booth/ Kellogg School Financial Trust Index provides a quarterly measure of the confidence Americans have in their financial institutions.[3] It shows that Americans' trust in banks is remarkably similar to Australians' trust in bank managers—around 33 per cent. While such surveys do not normally extend beyond the past thirty years, a reading of the media commentary of the 1930s or even the 1880s suggests that this perception is not a modern phenomenon. What is interesting is that increased public access to information, improved transparency of activities, and almost real-time exposure of misbehaviour has apparently done very little to change the perception for the better.

A CAUSE FOR DISTRUST

To better understand why the public has persistently rated the finance sector poorly for honesty and integrity, it might be instructive to compare the core professional characteristics of the health and education sectors with those of finance and business. It is worth bearing in mind that the surveys reflect the public's perception of, and their experience with, the finance sector. They do not necessarily provide an objective measure of ethical behaviour in finance. They are also limited to the public stakeholder. There are no similar surveys for the other stakeholders, like governments, regulators, corporations, other financial institutions, or even customers. It is therefore appropriate to start with the key characteristics that affect the profession's interaction with the public, rather than its equally important interactions with corporations or with other financial institutions.

Four key factors can be identified that are influential in contributing to the public's lack of trust in the ethics and integrity of the finance sector:

1. the complexity of the service
2. the information asymmetry between professionals and customers
3. the familiarity with the subject matter
4. the uncertainty of the outcome.

COMPLEXITY

Most people know little about the inner workings of the sectors which they engage for services, and therefore they may feel at a disadvantage when interacting. Some may even have a natural inclination to distrust the better-informed party. Such distrust may well be on the rise in an increasingly specialised environment where knowledge is ever so rapidly accumulated by experts—although access to information has certainly led to more-informed customers, if they are interested in doing their research.

In relation to the finance sector, there have been efforts to boost confidence to engage with it. Such efforts include financial literacy programs, informative websites (populated by regulators or an ombudsman), and educative information distributed by financial institutions. Imparting or sharing knowledge can enhance the relationship with the public. Attempting to restrict (and potentially abuse) knowledge, on the other hand, can further strain the relations between the sector and the public.

If the knowledge is considered too complicated or specialist to communicate, then a sector needs to convince the public it is using that knowledge for the benefit of both individuals and the public more generally. The health profession is the standard-bearer here, justifying its persistent high ranking on the ethics scale. But even that profession occasionally suffers from a lack of trust, particularly when it fails to communicate the 'knowledge-for-good' argument. Consider, for example, the debate around stem-cell research, where the health sector failed to clearly communicate the benefits of using human embryonic stem cells in research to cure disease and alleviate suffering.

So is the finance sector perceived in relation to the knowledge which it holds? The level of knowledge and professional competence required to be successful in finance has increased exponentially in the past few decades. Comprehensive financial deregulation resulted in new waves of financial innovation and financial engineering. Rather than always explaining the innovative new assets and investment products to their customers, some banks instead have used and protected their inside knowledge as a valuable competitive tool. In some cases, what may seem as ever more complicated products are created and marketed to what could be perceived as an ever more disadvantaged clientele—not just institutional investors but retail clients as well. A 2017 Consumer Federation of America survey reflected this erosion of public knowledge of pivotal financial information (credit scores).[4]

The introduction of a range of mortgage products—from no-deposit, interest-only loans with offset account to mortgage-backed securities (MBSs)—has been quite illustrative of the problem. Tempted by lower monthly repayments, home-loan borrowers have not always realised that interest-only loans carry significant risk of underwater mortgages in overinflated real estate markets. (A mortgage is defined as underwater when the balance of the mortgage exceeds the market value of the property.) Likewise, the highly inventive MBS market allowed banks to transfer significant risks of portfolios of non-performing home loans. Their complexity confused and in some cases blindsided investors, rating agencies, regulators, and in some instances the banks themselves. It would appear that some MBS originators were either unable to explain the true nature of the assets, or deliberately withheld that information from the investors.

The change from predominantly plain-vanilla mortgages to mortgages with complicated bells and whistles attached was acknowledged as a positive by mortgage broker Leteisha Pileggi from Australian company Mortgage Choice: 'The days when home loans were a one-size-fits-all product are over. Thank goodness for that! In today's competitive market, lenders are increasingly coming up with new and exciting loan options and features. It's a plus for the industry and it's great news for Australian borrowers'.[5] Indeed, choice brings many benefits to borrowers and lenders alike. But a mortgage broker's duty to its clients requires a clear explanation of the differences between products, and the financial consequences of any arrangement.

ASYMMETRY

Through specialisation, finance professionals have become better informed and more skilled in interpreting and using information. That, of course, is no different to other sectors and professions; for example, health professionals. So why is it that an informational disadvantage can cause people to distrust financial advice while at the same time trusting GPs to make the right diagnosis and prescribe the appropriate medications? Surely GPs might also benefit from expensive treatments, or drugs from certain 'friendly' pharmaceutical companies. Well, to prevent this from happening, the medical profession is supervised by a number of external agencies, as well as being subject to professional self-regulation. The regulation includes strict educational and licensing requirements and controls the level of competition between health providers. So where the medical profession uses the accumulation of knowledge to deliver a better health service,[6] the finance profession has at times used its knowledge to improve its competitive position.

Future Fund managing director David Neal made this very point by comparing public trust in the financial services sector with trust in the health sector: 'When you visit the dentist, he or she has every financial incentive to drill a hole and fill it. But we trust that they won't ... The financial industry has failed to generate this trust. True professionalism is lacking'.[7]

Knowledge asymmetry easily translates into power asymmetry. The latter manifests itself through a complexity of transactions, lack of transparency, appearance of potential conflicts of interest, and gaps in access to legal justice. The 2016 Australian parliamentary inquiry into small business loans highlighted the almost complete asymmetry of power in the relationship between banks and small business borrowers. A similar power asymmetry seems to exist in insurance products.

Interestingly, much relevant information is nowadays publicly and instantaneously available. The internet (and more narrowly, Wikipedia) allows us to access previously proprietary information, including databases, manuals and instructions. The internet also provides explanations of complex concepts, comparisons of products and costs, and user-tailored advice. This could be seen to eliminate asymmetric information, but unfortunately that does not always happen. Instead, many people find themselves overwhelmed by an ocean of information, unable to discriminate between the sources of that information, with the resulting risk that they will rely on superficial (often inaccurate or unreliable) information. Ironically, despite the best legislative and regulatory efforts to enhance transparency through full disclosure, the mark is sometimes still missed. The 2015 research report *Too Long; Didn't Read: Enhancing General Insurance Disclosure*, by the Insurance Council of Australia, indicates that four in five customers do not read a product disclosure statement before buying an insurance policy.[8]

Asymmetric information is clearly not just about one party having privileged access to relevant information when others do not. It is also about the ability to sort, interpret and query that information, the access to networks to test and use the information, and the capacity to connect diverse sources (and historical records) of information.

FAMILIARITY

When considering the knowledge gap between the specialised professional and the public, it may be worth distinguishing between actual and perceived knowledge. The public may feel they have or at least should have financial knowledge, as it affects their daily lives. This is not necessarily so for medical, engineering or scientific knowledge, where the public's interaction with those professions is rare or remote.

But this is changing. Endowed with Wikipedia knowledge, the average person feels empowered to judge medical experts, teachers and scientists as much as their bank managers, to the point that they become suspicious of real trained experts if their advice or diagnosis does not match, for example, an online medical library. When customers interact with those experts, they come armed with preconceived opinions and solutions that can push the experts into defensive positions.

Finance has a head start in these 'public knowledge' stakes. Dedicated financial newspapers, regular (daily) media commentary and frequency of service use all contribute to a close familiarity with the subject matter. So many actions an individual takes on a daily basis have a financial aspect. We move money from our savings to our home loan accounts using internet banking; we swipe our credit cards when buying a coffee, use our smartphones to book and pay for an Uber ride. In a way, we have become mini-bankers in our own right. The transactions seem simple enough, leaving us to ponder why we need banks at all, why the need to pay such high executive salaries. A feeling that 'anybody could do this job' may explain the loss of respect.

UNCERTAINTY

One of the core functions of the finance sector is financial intermediation by transforming short-term small savings deposits into long-term large (business, home) loans. In exchange for interest payments, depositors (savers) postpone consumption and are exposed to the risk that the borrowers will not repay their loans. History has delivered multiple examples of banks failing to repay their depositors, so this is not just a hypothetical outcome. Following the bank runs in the 1933 Depression, many countries introduced a deposit insurance scheme that protected depositors' funds, although not always in full.

Since the hyperinflation and stagflation days of the 1970s, monetary authorities (central banks) have successfully targeted low levels of inflation. In response to the global financial crisis, most major economies adopted a policy of quantitative easing to stimulate the economy and prevent a recession. Both policies have driven down official cash rates and, as a consequence, returns on saving deposits are now at all-time lows, with some countries offering *negative* interest rates. In that counterintuitive scenario, lenders and depositors are prepared to pay for the privilege of investing, despite being exposed to possible repayment default, while borrowers are paid for taking out a loan.

Increasingly, therefore, depositors have been looking for better return-generating investment options than low interest savings deposits and fixed income assets. Banks and investment managers have responded by offering a wider range of investment schemes, derivative securities and managed funds. Many of these investment opportunities carry significantly higher risk and are not protected. Some have had disappointing outcomes, and investors have sought to apportion blame for their losses. Of course, there is the randomness of investment outcomes that can undermine even the most competent financial advice.

WHAT PRICE ECONOMIC GROWTH?

The four features of interaction with finance described above serve to explain some of the public's distrust in finance ethics. But individuals still engage with financial services, and for very good reasons. While not always (or rarely) acknowledged, finance plays a crucial role in driving economic development, delivering economic growth and encouraging household prosperity. Is the latest financial crisis and persistent unethical behaviours in the banking sector the inevitable price we have to pay?

For the past four centuries, the establishment of corporations and financial markets has unleashed and then pushed along global economic growth, lifting people worldwide from extreme poverty. Despite the Club of Rome think tank's doomsday scenarios indicating the limits to growth,[9] many developing countries (China and India in particular) have been able to transform themselves into emerging market economies, with a rapidly growing middle class and a burgeoning finance sector. Financial services have undoubtedly responded to increased demand from growth, as Nobel laureate Robert E Lucas argued in a 1988 paper modelling economic development.[10] A subsequent review by Ross Levine, a professor of economics at UC Berkeley, suggested it is equally valid to claim that financial institutions have significantly contributed to that growth.[11] In the aftermath of the global financial crisis, professors Stephen Cecchetti and Enisse Kharroub, of the Brandeis International Business School and the Bank for International Settlements respectively, made the case that the positive contribution by the finance sector to economic growth would start to diminish and turn negative beyond a certain level of economic growth.[12]

Regardless of the net contribution to growth, the ability to efficiently buy and sell, save, invest and borrow has facilitated economic activity, spread economic prosperity and raised living standards. That is not an abstract notion, but one that directly affects each and every one of us on a daily basis. In our quest for economic improvement we have embraced finance in so many ways that we have become increasingly dependent on it. That dependence means that we increasingly rely on the financial system (and its institutions), but importantly that it is necessary for the individuals employed by the sector to do the right thing. We have to place our trust in its functioning and objectives. Unfortunately, this also exposes us to its flaws and failures, including unethical behaviour.

As the Bank of England's chief economist, Andy Haldane, said:

> ... it's about why this decline in trust of bankers should matter not just to the banks themselves, but for the whole economy ... There's more and more research suggesting trust is a vital ingredient in economic growth ... [where] high levels of trust and co-operation are associated with higher economic growth. Put differently, a lack of trust jeopardises one of finance's key societal functions—higher growth.[13]

And while growth may be a necessary condition for the improvement of societal welfare, it does not seem to be a sufficient condition. The economic transformations of the past three decades (Eastern Europe, South-East Asia, Latin America) indicate that volatility, inequality and unethical behaviour often accompany strong economic growth.

DISRUPTION

Just as higher (expected) returns can be achieved by taking bigger risks, with strong economic growth comes volatility. We see this most vividly in emerging economies with growth rates in excess of 5 per cent per annum, like India and China, and in commodity economies like Australia. High economic growth is occasionally punctuated by short, sharp and deep recessions and market crises. Trying to keep pace with economic growth, whole industry sectors come under pressure. Buckling under excessive demand for their output, manufacturers and miners face supply constraints, labour shortages and infrastructure deficiencies. When these constraints become binding, contracts become void, financing disappears and companies default.

In a story about the volatility of China's emerging stock market, *Sydney Morning Herald* journalist Richard Frost noted:

> As is typical in a … market dominated by individual investors, pinpointing the reasons for the sudden loss of confidence is hard. Traders have cited the securities regulator's increased scrutiny on irregularities in the market … and fears that a strengthening economy will prompt more tightening by the central bank … The recent declines represent a swift reversal. Just a week ago the Shanghai Composite was at heights not seen for 15 months …[14]

Regarding the significant market fluctuations characteristic of high-growth economies, how much (if any) of that volatility is due to financial institutions? There is certainly evidence that banks fuel economic growth by increasingly extending (in some cases ever more risky) loans to opportunistically gain market share in what could be considered overheated economies. An economy is considered overheated when sustained high levels of economic growth start to cause inflation and distort the efficient allocation of capital. When capacity constraints are breached, regulators intervene by tightening interest rates and increasing capital requirements. Banks then go into what could be interpreted as 'survival mode', limiting the supply of new (or rollover) loans and calling risky loans (that is, demanding early repayment). Business credit then disappears and the market disturbance can spill over into the real economy, causing a contracting of business growth and possibly triggering a recession.[15] This phenomenon was never more starkly illustrated than in the global financial crisis.

In January 2017, *Washington Post* journalist Steven Arons wrote about how Deutsche Bank reached a settlement with the US Justice Department over its handling of MBSs before 2008, resolving one of its biggest litigation risks. US Attorney-General Loretta Lynch commented: 'This resolution holds Deutsche Bank accountable for its illegal conduct and irresponsible lending practices, which caused serious and lasting damage to investors and the American public … Deutsche Bank did not merely mislead investors. It contributed directly to an international financial crisis'.[16]

INEQUALITY

The spoils from economic growth benefit everybody, what we might call a Pareto-improving outcome (a Pareto improvement occurs when a change in the economy, such as growth, improves someone's welfare without harming anyone else's welfare). Extreme poverty is undeniably diminishing, and poverty itself has been redefined. Yet, at the same time, income inequality is becoming more severe. In his bestselling text *Capital in the Twenty-First Century*, Thomas Piketty, professor of economics at L'ecole des Hautes Etudes en Sciences Sociales, writes that the richest '1%' continue to take an even larger share of the growing pie.[17] Fairness and justice appear to be going begging in order to achieve and maintain economic growth.

Two questions arise from observing the increasing concentration of wealth accumulation. First, should we be concerned about inequality? After all, if everyone improves, is that not more important? From an ethical perspective, distributional justice is vital. Looking at the divergent experiences of China and India, it is hard to escape the conclusion that excessive inequality is morally unsustainable and just not ethical or right.

The second question is whether the finance sector is contributing to the widening inequality. In a 2016 report by the Organisation for Economic Co-operation and Development (OECD) entitled *Finance, Growth and Inequality*, Boris Cournede and Oliver Denk suggested that finance may indeed have exacerbated income inequality:

> There are few financial sector employees in low-income brackets and many higher up in the income distribution. The strong presence of financial sector workers among top earners is justified as long as very high productivity underpins their earnings. However, our ... investigations show that financial firms pay wages well above what employees with similar profiles earn in other sectors. The premium is especially large for top earners.
>
> ... Banks generally concentrate their lending on higher-income borrowers. Credit is twice as unequally distributed as *household* income ... This may reduce credit risk, but it also means that well-off people have greater opportunities than the poor to borrow money and fund profitable projects. In this way, lenders are likely to amplify inequalities in income, consumption and opportunities.

... Stock market wealth is concentrated among high-income households who thus get most of the income and capital gains generated through capital markets.[18]

A lack of access to—or even the denial of—banking services excludes significant parts of society from effective economic participation, in turn excluding them from participating in the benefits of economic growth.

You might think that this is mostly a concern in poor developing economies, and that their economic development will eventually resolve the issue. Indeed, in its 2015 report *Measuring Financial Inclusion around the World*, the World Bank suggested that financial inclusion was improving: 'From 2011 [to] 2014, 700 million people became account holders at banks, other financial institutions, or mobile money service providers, and the number of "unbanked" individuals dropped 20 per cent to 2 billion adults ...'[19] Technological advances certainly contribute to this improvement.[20] However, '2 billion' still suggests an enormous moral obligation for the global financial system.

And yes, limited access to formal banking services is most pertinent in countries like Cambodia, but even in a developed economy like Australia, about 15 per cent of the population is 'severely excluded' from accessing basic financial services. According to a story by Ian Rogers on BankingDay in 2011:

A new assessment of the level of the 'unbanked' in Australia puts the proportion of the population excluded from access to everyday financial services at 0.8 per cent. A further 14.8 per cent of people are 'severely excluded', the study found. Though practically all this second group had a bank account most lacked both a credit card and general insurance.

... only 43.4 per cent of the adult population could be considered to be financially 'included', with access to all three everyday financial products.[21]

While financial exclusion is itself explained by poverty, it also perpetuates and deepens poverty, and increases income inequality.

UNETHICAL BEHAVIOURS

In a rapidly growing economy, the finance sector quickly expands. When opportunity abounds, unscrupulous financial providers can be drawn like moths to a flame. With promises of higher returns, based on underestimated risks, their offers can be too tempting for investors who do not want to miss out on the possibility of financial gain.

Emerging economies can present a difficult environment due to concerns about transparency, reliability of information, and information asymmetry, which can be high. Established reputations may be absent, and transactions based on trust in an individual rather than in an organisation. In some cases, unsophisticated (and poorly funded) regulatory structures and loopholes in legal protection essentially mean that customers are on their own. Unfortunately, examples of ethical misconduct abound, and the culprits often get away with it due to ineffective regulatory or legal recourse. The cost of unethical conduct can be staggering for economies in transition.

However, even developed economies with sophisticated financial systems and institutions can struggle with systemic unethical behaviour in a rapidly growing finance sector. And again, the cost of that behaviour is significant. Roger McCormick, as director of the Conduct Costs Project (CCP) Research Foundation at the London School of Economics, provided a (lower) estimate of this cost based on public data from the world's largest banks.[22] The now independent CCP Research Foundation regularly updates this project. Its purpose is to make transparent unethical practice in the finance sector. As Adele Ferguson wrote in *The Sydney Morning Herald* in 2016: 'The Conduct Costs Project has put a figure of $419 billion on the global cost of financial misconduct between 2009 and 2014—tallying up all court-enforced penalties, settlements and regulatory fines forked out by financial institutions ...'[23]

And this is just the direct cost to the (major) financial institutions. It does not measure the indirect costs to the financial system, nor the ongoing cost of distrust. Even a proven and trusted regulatory (and legal) system may not be up to the task. In April 2017, after investigating the reason behind the delayed news release of an enforceable undertaking by the Australian Securities & Investments Commission (ASIC), *Australian* journalist Ben Butler wrote: 'The documents reinforce the impression of

[ASIC] as a "timid, hesitant regulator, too ready and willing to accept uncritically the assurances of a large institution" delivered in a scathing June 2014 Senate economics committee ...'[24]

MAKING FINANCE BETTER

Despite these shortcomings and misgivings, the benefits to society of an efficient and ethical financial system should be obvious. But where are the champions? Who will speak up for finance? Examples of unethical behaviour and a lack of professionalism in responding to these cases can conspire to create a tense relationship between finance and the public. When confronted by evidence of unethical behaviour, the response of CEOs and their media liaison officers can be denial or a downplaying of the evidence. In some cases, a whistleblower has been ostracised. This does not seem to be a productive way forward.

Can we retain the benefits of an efficient finance sector while improving its reputation and re-establishing trust and ethical behaviour as the foundation on which all services are provided? To answer this question, we need to identify the 'hot spots' of unethical behaviour. The next few chapters will take a closer look at finance practice and a range of ethical issues of relevance to the sector. A brief review of the theoretical ethical foundations will give some guidance in understanding how ethics can influence and shape the decision-making of all individuals working in finance.

ETHICAL POSITIONS

Individuals working in finance will have to make many business decisions—some minor regarding their ethical consequences, some causing major ethical concerns. Should a home loan be approved even though there is concern about the applicant's capacity to repay? Should a high-risk investment opportunity be recommended to a client who is about to retire? Should life insurance be sold to a couple who just lost their home in a bushfire? The answers to such questions could be derived from personal values and principles. However, some may argue that institutional principles trump personal principles where work-related decisions are concerned.

Many institutions have vision and mission statements and a set of values of their own. These are typically enshrined in a code of conduct that sets standards and informs workplace behaviours. Accordingly, decision-making on the questions raised above may become routine, made almost without consideration or further thought. Few employees may question or reflect on their professional code on a regular basis, if at all. A well-functioning code becomes a mantra, defining the institutional culture and entrenching 'the way we do business'. Over time, however, some individuals may wonder about what sacrifices they have made while suspending their personal principles in order to adhere to institutional codes or practices.

If an employer's code of conduct is a comprehensive guide to decision-making, should the answer to specific questions depend on the type of institution you work for? For example, would you behave differently if you worked for an investment bank on Wall Street than for a mortgage broker or financial adviser in a small regional town? Or are all financial institutions fundamentally alike in their aspirations, duties and obligations?

To help navigate ethical decision-making, we can use a simple, two-dimensional decision-making framework that generates four distinct ethical positions. One dimension pits principles against consequences, while the other dimension pits institutional decision-making against personal decision-making. The framework is not so much prescriptive as it is descriptive. It may help individuals understand why people and institutions make certain decisions and how they are justified.

UTILITARIANISM—THE LEDGER OF CONSEQUENCES

Consider a microfinance organisation planning to expand its operations. By raising capital from hedge funds, many new microloans can be provided, with the potential to lift many more families and communities out of poverty than would be possible by relying on philanthropy alone. This appears to be a good outcome. However, it might well be that these loans are extended at interest rates that are significantly beyond the borrowers' capacity to repay. This would then be considered a bad outcome for the borrowers. To make matters worse for borrowers in arrears, the hedge fund could also impose conditions on investment; for example, a much stricter recovery of non-performing loans.

One common ethics theory, utilitarianism, argues that the decision to accept or reject hedge fund investment should be based on the consequences of that decision—trading off all the good outcomes against all the bad outcomes. If one were to tally up all the good outcomes and subtract all the bad outcomes, and still end up good in aggregate, then utilitarian ethics tell us that the ethical decision is to go ahead with the injection of hedge fund capital. This, of course, is colloquially described as 'the ends justifying the means'.

Most business ethics texts start with utilitarianism. This order of treatment could be seen to reflect utility theory's popularity in business decision-making practice over the past 200 years. A decade ago, Shane Premeaux, professor of marketing at McNeese State University in Louisiana, said he thought practitioners still relied heavily on utilitarian ethics.[25] Outcomes-based ethics allow the decision-maker to invoke experience and present observable evidence on outcomes, rather than rely on immovable duties and principles with uncertain consequences, which can lack verifiable outcomes. If we want to achieve something important, such as lifting people out of poverty, we justify our actions based on measurable outcomes. This argument resonates particularly with economists and business professionals trained as what could be termed rational, expected utility maximising agents.

However, there are some problems with utilitarian ethics as a framework for ethical decision-making. The theory—focused on the greatest good/happiness for the greatest number of people—is somewhat silent on whose interests (or outcomes) should be considered in determining whether an action is deemed ethical. Utilitarianism is bookended by two extreme positions. One is that of the decision-maker who merely pursues their own personal gain, ignoring everyone else's, which is known as ethical egoism. The eighteenth-century economist and philosopher Adam Smith's propagation of the pursuit of self-interest to best fulfil the greater good, fits with this position.[26] But that premise requires many assumptions—for example, perfect competition, rational utility-maximising behaviour, and the absence of externalities, among others—that we cannot reasonably take for granted in the real world. The other extreme arises when a decision-maker considers everyone's gains except their own, which is known as ethical altruism. Both positions should be seen as rather extreme versions of utilitarian ethics, with few adherents to support either as acceptable and practical ethical decision-making.

However, in-between these extreme variants is the position known as utilitarian ethics, where it is less straightforward to determine whose outcomes should be part of the aggregation. At a minimum, should everyone included at least be directly involved? In the microfinance example, this would mean the principals of the microfinance institution, the hedge fund investors, and the borrowers. But does it stop there? What if the higher interest rates filter through to other loans and impact other borrowers as well? What about the village merchants benefiting from an improved economy? Those externalities suggest a much broader coverage of interests, including everyone indirectly impacted. Of course, this does not even include the benefit that all of mankind derives from eradicating poverty.

Once it has been determined who to include in the measurement of aggregate benefits, there are still concerns to be addressed. How does one measure and compare outcomes for the identified stakeholders? Is it a profit or a cost that can be expressed in dollars? Is it the quality of life that we might express in years of life expectancy? Economics might have you believe that we can express all gains and losses in terms of (monetary) utility. This can sometimes lead to confused policy-makers. Consider, for example, the economist who uses a utility-maximising framework to quantify what it would 'cost' to encourage graduate accountants to accept a job in poor, remote communities in urgent need of accounting and financial advisory services. The dollar premium over an equivalent city accounting job captures the perceived cost of remoteness, the lack of educational and health facilities, and many other disadvantages. Unfortunately, paying that premium may not incentivise an accountant to relocate to the remote community, as no amount of financial subsidy could compensate for the lack of, for example, childcare facilities. Nonetheless, most applications of utilitarian ethics do adopt such rationales.

Perhaps even more complicated is the question of how to allocate weight to specific outcomes of stakeholders. One might ask if some stakeholders are more important than others. How do you weigh the economic advancement of a village against the potential loss of life? Some outcomes might simply be considered unacceptable, or even make the decision illegal. More subtly, economists recognise that the marginal utility of a small profit for someone living on the poverty line is many times larger than the marginal utility of that same small profit for someone with substantial life savings. Yet many decision-makers would judge those profits equivalent when aggregating the gains of a decision.

This dilemma is perhaps best illustrated by the practice of payday lending. Payday lenders extend small loans to borrowers who are in financial distress, or lack short-term access to cash, until their next payday, at what are considered to be very high interest rates. The practice is generally condemned as predatory and unethical, yet from a utilitarian point of view it may have its merits. In 2010, *Guardian* journalist Faisel Rahman quoted a report which

> suggests that data from the US finds that access to payday finance helps people to manage short-term credit flows and can stave off financial crisis. It also suggests that banning the service or imposing rate caps in two US states had resulted in more complaints about debt problems and higher rates of bankruptcies.[27]

Utilitarian ethics is remarkably silent on rights, fairness and justice in distributing the benefits of a business decision. It is not necessarily incompatible with these concepts; it is just agnostic. In its purest form, a decision rule based on the balance of good over bad outcomes does not preclude characterising a decision as ethical when it generates a number of losers. In practice, individuals have certain (some of them inalienable) rights by law which could be reconciled with utilitarian ethics through constrained utility maximisation. Utilitarians would also point out that justice and fairness do not necessarily require equality in outcomes. Differences in outcomes could be proportional to effort, contribution or need. In any case, if aggregate utility is computed by weighing marginal utilities, then diminishing marginal utility will favour ethical business outcomes that are more egalitarian.

Market proponents would argue that utilitarian ethics is in fact merely market forces leading to Pareto-optimal efficient outcomes. Pareto-optimality is an allocation of resources that cannot possibly be improved for one individual without making at least one other individual worse off. Again, this does not necessarily lead to a fair outcome for all stakeholders. For example, it may be hard to justify the privatisation of a public energy utility where the biggest beneficiaries are senior management, while the taxpayer only receives a minor (and temporary) energy price reduction—even though the outcome is technically Pareto-optimal.

DUTY—UPHOLDING PRINCIPLES

Utilitarian ethics might be appealing to many business decision-makers, but they are rarely used in isolation. In practice, outcome-based decision-making is commonly counterbalanced by principle-based decision-making. As outcome-based decision-making depends on expected outcomes, it is worth remembering that actual outcomes may diverge from what was expected. Time and again, the market delivers unanticipated consequences of actions that were morally acceptable at the time, but in hindsight no longer are. On many occasions, this reflects the fact that the decision-maker was unable to grasp the possible externalities of the decision. Whenever this happens—and it usually does during a recession, a market crash or a financial crisis—people and businesses can be seen to revert to principles to restore stability to the system. Not making further loans to people who cannot afford repayment (that is, rejecting actions on principled moral grounds) is a standard response in these circumstances. What was previously considered an acceptable risk, given the expected outcomes, may no longer qualify as such based on the minimum requirements of creditworthiness and trust.

Issuing credit cards to customers who lack evidence of creditworthiness appears reckless. Yet some banks encourage their customers to increase their credit card limits despite their repayments already being in arrears. Strong economic conditions with steady wages growth mean that these high-risk customers manage to stay ahead of default, and the decision to increase credit limits therefore might be ethical for a utilitarian. But if the economy takes a turn for the worse, these customers can lose their jobs, face severe indebtedness, and have no choice but to file for personal bankruptcy or be forced into stringent repayment plans. One would then be left to wonder if those banks would have been so forthcoming had they foreseen such outcomes.

In the wake of the subprime mortgage disaster that prompted the global financial crisis, some banks concluded that they had been (and still were) exposed to hitherto unforeseen risks. This provides an interesting illustration of a transition from outcome-based to principle-based decision-making. With abundant credit and the ever lower cost of funds in the 1990s, some banks increasingly extended mortgages to low- or uncertain-income households who were previously constrained to renting. When computing the aggregate expected utility of these subprime mortgages, the banks decided that the net benefits outweighed the increased risk of defaults. All kinds of shortcuts—including waivers of documented payment capacity, or the need to buy mortgage insurance, or minimum deposit requirements—were allowed by the banks to ensure that they could maintain their mortgage market share. This can be seen as a utilitarian ethical justification.

These banks, and even the regulators on occasion, did not necessarily foresee the simultaneous housing glut (jeopardising loan-to-value, or LTV, ratios) and business cycle contraction (jeopardising employment opportunities) that led to a domino effect of mortgage defaults spreading across the world. Regulators, and then the banks themselves, concluded that the subprime mortgages should never have been extended in the first place. The necessary documentation, borrower deposits and mortgage insurance were all reinstituted and income thresholds were set considerably higher. Risk-taking by the banks was therefore significantly diminished, with the consequence that some low-income households now struggle to secure home loans. As many of these households may, in fact, fulfil their contractual loan repayments, is this a fair or ethical outcome?

At first glance, it may appear that principles-based ethical decision-making, which is known as duty ethics, is somewhat inflexible and traditional, and could contravene market economics. In short, it could be seen to stymie economic growth and financial advancement. But it can also provide safeguards, setting boundaries around an unbridled market economy. It is worth recalling that efficient market economics requires many assumptions, most of which are rarely met in practice. Imperfect markets (a less than competitive banking system), irrational borrowers (taking 120 per cent LTV mortgages when property prices are expected to fall) and many externalities (US counties buying MBSs originated in Iceland) are, unfortunately somewhat symptomatic of the modern financial system.

Most financial institutions concerned with building trust and having a good reputation have public vision, mission and values statements that espouse the way they will operate. These statements suggest that duty ethics has a role to play. Such statements may refer to certain duties imposed by a social licence to operate as a bank or other financial institution. In this context, an ethical decision is one that conforms to a rational, generally recognised duty.

In 2015, the UK-based Co-operative Bank relaunched its ethical policy, after having been the first bank to introduce one in 1992. As reported in the *Manchester Evening News*, chief executive Niall Booker recommitted the bank to a number of 'duties' underpinning the new code of ethics:

> The Co-operative Bank has today launched an expanded Ethical Policy based on the views of more than 74 000 customers and colleagues ...
> As a result the Bank will not finance any companies or organisations that are involved in irresponsible gambling and pay day loans. It will also be extending its commitment not to finance companies or organisations which do not responsibly pay tax to include the UK or elsewhere.[28]

Duties are understood in two ways, first by reason, which the eighteenth-century German philosopher Immanuel Kant called the test of the categorical imperative whereby a decision is universally accepted or obeyed.[29] They are also understood by intuition, which the twentieth-century Scottish philosopher William Ross called the common sense test.[30] Fidelity, gratitude, reparation and non-maleficence are just some examples of the duties that may inform ethical decision-making.

In practice, these duties translate into rules and behaviours stipulated in a code of conduct. Ross' common sense suggests that it is hard to disagree with codes that are general in nature. Unfortunately, ascribing business practices entirely to duty ethics is not without problems. First, as the list of duties can be comprehensive, and each duty may in turn consider specific, unique actions, it is not impossible for a complicated business transaction to involve the simultaneous resolution of multiple duties. There is no guarantee—or in-built structure that ensures—that these duties will be aligned. Second, duty ethics does not look for good outcomes, but rather for good intentions. Whether a business is indeed run on good intentions is difficult to observe, let alone monitor. While the public has certain expectations of banks' behaviour, it seems that they mostly prioritise outcomes within a constraining set of absolute (moral) rules. A proclamation by financial institutions that they 'did the morally right thing' might appeal to duty ethicists, but it is unlikely to appease the customers who have just lost their retirement income because the superannuation fund refuses on principle to buy derivatives.

While utilitarianism, when properly applied, 'weighs' individuals' utility in the aggregation, thereby possibly achieving fairness and justice, duty ethicists would argue that it does not seriously account for differences in individual circumstances. According to John Rawls, the twentieth-century American moral and political philosopher, egalitarianism argues that utilitarianism inevitably favours one's self-interest over someone else's.[31] It takes the principle of social justice to find truly mutually beneficial outcomes. True, social justice does not necessarily require outcome equality. The libertarian entitlement theory of another twentieth-century American philosopher, Robert Nozick, makes this clear.[32] A typical ethical duty could be to respect property rights. Accordingly, a distribution of outcomes is then morally just when every stakeholder is entitled to the property they possess. In any case, how exactly to achieve a just society may differ greatly according to different individuals and sectors.

VIRTUE—ARISTOTLE'S HOMECOMING

While the institutional environment determines much of how we behave and operate in the workplace, individuals are also driven by their own personal ethics. For a start, our 'character' has probably influenced our choice of profession, our choice of desired employer, and our likelihood of getting employed. When human resources managers talk about 'cultural fit', they are sometimes referring to a match between institutional and personal ethics. This term has been problematic, allowing for conscious and unconscious bias in recruitment. Invariably, however, personal ethics spill over into our approach to work.

In a 2004 opinion piece, Kevin Burns captured this notion of personal ethics infiltrating the workplace:

> There may come a time in our lives when we are faced with an ethics question. The funny thing about ethics though, is that we never really notice our personal ethics until they come into conscious conflict with something we don't agree with. We know what the 'right thing' is.

The 'right thing' is a set of values instilled in each of us. We know right from wrong. We know about honour and integrity and we, for the most part, will usually not do the thing that hurts others. We understand our own values and ethics.[33]

As with the utilitarian and duty ethics theories, it is important to distinguish decisions based on intentions from those based on outcomes. Whereas institutional ethics address the question of which actions are ethically right, personal ethics address the question of what kind of person one should be. Virtue ethics also focus on the latter in order to help individuals lead a good life; that is, a life where virtue rules and is rewarded accordingly. According to this theory, good decisions are considered reflective of (and productive in developing) character, which sustains traits that lead to a good life. Those character traits are culturally acknowledged; for example, courage, justice, honesty and generosity.

In recent times there has been a shift in the business ethics discourse from the institutional to the personal, and in particular to virtue ethics. This heralds a homecoming of sorts for Aristotelian ethics.[34] Having been the hallmark of ethics since 350 BCE, Aristotle's ethics theory was sidelined in the seventeenth century by utilitarian ethics following the introduction of the modern corporation. The creation and acceptance of the corporation could be considered the single most important organisational innovation in business history. It fundamentally changed the relationship between business and ethics. The move from craftsmen, partnerships and family business to modern-day corporations cut the ties between ownership and management, and limited an owner's liability regarding unfavourable business outcomes. There are still many family businesses and small enterprises, of course, but there are also many registered corporations. The legal features of such corporations have depersonalised ethics, inaugurating a new paradigm of institutionalised ethics. It is perhaps not surprising that this period coincided with an abundance of ethical writing by utilitarians such as Adam Smith,[35] the eighteenth-century philosopher and social reformer Jeremy Bentham,[36] the nineteenth-century political economist John Stuart Mill,[37] and many others, in an attempt to make sense of the corporations' ethical behaviour in an age of industrialisation.

We have now entered an era when the public's discontent with corporations has become increasingly widespread and at times virulent.

Discontent calls out globally operating corporations that seemingly answer to no jurisdiction, CEOs with excessive remuneration packages regardless of performance, and shareholders who cannot be held accountable for corporate actions. With increasing scrutiny of unethical behaviour, utilitarian ethics has at times been found wanting. CEOs who point to codes of conduct and company culture initiatives are an indication that the pendulum may have swung too far, and too often, towards utilitarian ethics. Basic virtues such as honesty, compassion and integrity are too often sacrificed for the greater good of economic growth.

Enter virtue ethics: the theory of doing things right, not in excess nor in deficiency. A typical illustration of virtue ethics in business is whistleblowing, whereby an employee alerts the outside world to unethical practices within the company they work for. A utilitarian would argue that the whistleblower needs to assess the consequences of their actions before deciding to go public. Virtue ethics, on the other hand, requires that the action is based on virtuous personal behaviour. The list of virtues is as long as the list of duties—a virtue arises if it helps in building good character. In the case of whistleblowing, the virtue would be the courage to speak out, the midpoint of the two equally bad vices of cowardice (not daring to speak out) and rashness (speaking out too quickly). The personal consequences of whistleblowing— being vilified, losing one's job, ensuring the company's future ethical behaviour—do not necessarily influence the virtuous person.

The application of this theory faces similar difficulties as duty ethics. First, it is possible that two virtues will lead to conflicting actions—the inevitable trade-off between loyalty and integrity in the case of whistleblowing, for example. Second, virtue ethics does not look for good outcomes for all, or even for good intentions towards all. A particularly negative interpretation of virtue ethics could lead to a conclusion of ethical egoism whereby individuals only take actions that build their character. That was never Aristotle's intention, as vanity would be considered a vice. Nonetheless, there may be a certain uneasy feeling about the good life as the single deciding factor for ethical behaviour.

RELATIVIST—UPHOLDING COMMUNITY

The ethical theories already covered have separated personal from institutional ethics to explain how we behave in the workplace.

However, it is not just the workplace where we engage with other individuals. Our social interactions extend to the personal sphere, where we belong to, and participate in, various communities. The final theory in the ethical theory framework recognises that ethics is learnt in the context of the community we live and work in. Relativist ethics prioritises the context over the individual, or the institution, in motivating morally right actions. That said, community values and norms change and evolve and may differ across communities. This reality implies that there is no objectively ethical right or wrong at any one time or in any one place.

A 2012 article by Alvin Lim of *The Straits Times* illustrates how (Asian) relativist ethics differs from (Western) utilitarian ethics. Lim quoted the executive chairman of the Singaporean business Banyan Tree Holdings, Ho Kwon Ping, as saying: 'Singapore has been trying to move towards a [relativist] ethic, as opposed to the adversarial approach of Western business methods'. The chairman then used corporate social responsibility (CSR) as an example:

> Western management teaching would be that CSR is good … because it helps the bottom line … and the money still goes back to shareholders … That should not be the reason … if all stakeholders are just as important, then practising CSR is a core mission … not a sideshow.[38]

Ethical relativism acknowledges that there is value in the utilitarian, duty and virtue theories in different measures at different times, places and contexts. Ethical transitions from virtue to utilitarian to duty, and back to virtue, demonstrate that social norms have changed significantly over time. Morally acceptable business practice in the nineteenth century was decidedly different from what is morally acceptable in the twenty-first century. When engaging in international business, it is also clear that norms are vastly different in a geographical sense. What is a morally acceptable practice in Senegal may be morally objectionable in Japan, and vice versa. Or, on a smaller scale, we might observe that rural business practices are vastly different from urban business practices. We could hypothesise about whether these norms are expected to converge over time, but that is not particularly helpful for decision-making in the present.

Ethical relativism takes place, time, community and culture as the setting for ethical learning. Rather than pursuing individual character traits in virtue ethics, personal ethical development is instead derived from the community of which the individual is part. Individuals can only aspire to develop their personal moral principles by partaking in, and contributing to, their ethically evolving communities, rather than attempting to do this in isolation. Learning and advancing the ethics of a community makes this a forward-looking theory, focused on improving communal ethical norms.

As with the other three theories, ethical relativism is not without shortcomings. First, whereas the others give reasonably clear guidance on ethically right or wrong decisions and actions, this theory is agnostic. It may seem intuitively appealing to allow for business practice to be informed by all four theories where suitable. But in doing so, the theory ignores the existence of universal ethical principles. Second, from a workplace perspective, ethical relativism ignores who has the right to make decisions and set the rules. Whose subjective ethics will ultimately determine how the institution conducts its business? In all likelihood, those norms will be set by senior management. Third, we are all part of many communities—town, religion, club, society, employer and so on. Some overlap and are ethically aligned, but many have their own specific moral norms. That leads to moral ambiguity, where the rules are no longer clear.

CONCLUSION

Trust is a fragile commodity. It requires constant maintenance and is hard to recover once lost. The finance sector conducts business on the basis of trust, yet the public regularly expresses a lack of trust in the ethics and integrity of finance. Whether public opinion is justified or not, the reputational cost of a lack of trust can be significant. That cost is borne by the financial institutions and their stakeholders, and the public. In the last ten years or so, the finance sector has become increasingly aware of the need to better manage its reputation. The move from a purely utilitarian ethical position to a more balanced ethical position that also considers duties and virtues, based on banking's social licence, is a clear signal of that change.

2

BETTER DAYS
The Social Contract
Clare Payne

A MOVE TO PROFESSIONALISM

While some working in finance lament the loss of trust and professionalism in the sector, others believe bankers and financiers should never have laid claim to being part of a profession. The global financial crisis of 2007–08, ongoing cases of fraud and ethical lapses in the finance sector have led regulators, associations and organisations to consider what constitutes a profession, and how they might formalise their standing as such.

A profession must be distinguished from the more colloquial reference to being 'professional', which most often implies being well presented, articulate and courteous in a business environment. A profession, and the professional who operates within it, are subject to more rigorous and distinct standards than mere professionalism. However, the definition of a profession can vary, as it is subject to disagreement.

Commonly cited elements of a profession are as follows:

- *A profession contains a specialised body of knowledge:* This technical knowledge is derived from research, education and training.
- *A profession engages in self-regulation:* Professions have considerable control over their own work, mostly through professional organisations that set standards for practice and processes for disciplining those who violate them.
- *Professions have a commitment to public service:* The knowledge of those in a profession serves an important social need, and there is a commitment to using that knowledge for the benefit of all.
- *A profession adheres to ethical standards:* Generally, a code of ethics will govern activities, requiring behaviour and practices beyond the personal moral obligations of an individual.

'The professional', then, is a member of a profession as it is defined. They are subject to codes and standards and, importantly, are held individually accountable for their actions when representing their profession.

The social compact of professions is often referenced, referring to an implicit agreement with society. Dr Simon Longstaff, executive director of The Ethics Centre, identifies that 'while the market satisfies customer's wants in the legitimate pursuit of self-interest, the professional subordinates their self-interest in the service of the interests of others, notably the public interest'.[1]

As the finance sector pursues a greater professional standing, the elements of training and self-regulation present an easier proposition for it. However, recognising and understanding the social contract between finance and society is a bigger issue, one that is likely to involve the challenging of current underlying and accepted principles of finance and financial markets. In addition, some would claim that engaging individuals, many of whom are well into their careers, to adopt new practices and have a new outlook is a nigh impossible task for a sector that experienced a swelling of staff numbers following the heady days of Wall Street in the 1980s, immortalised so well by the fictional character of Gordon Gekko in the 1987 film *Wall Street*.

It is interesting to note that while a group of sheep is a flock and a group of wolves is a pack, there is no name for a group of geckos.

This is because they do not in fact form groups in the wild.[2] Perhaps this is symbolic of the challenge the finance sector now faces as it attempts to raise the standards of a sector that stretches from financial planning to trading to investment banking, with each area tending to see itself as distinct from all the others, even though the public may perceive otherwise.

TRUSTING THE PROFESSIONAL

Gaining and upholding the trust of others should be the goal of any individual who cares about their work, and any organisation that wants to establish itself as a legitimate operator in financial markets. For a profession, trust is essential for maintaining its standing and social licence to operate.

However, trust is merely the result of other factors such as reputation, experience and the relationships that are formed. Ethics can be seen as the essential thread that must pass through all practices and behaviours in order for the desired outcome of trust to be achieved.

A relationship of trust can be seen to involve the following:
- A party is willing to rely on the actions of another.
- The situation is directed to the future.
- There is some abandonment of control by the trusting party over the actions performed by the other party.

The complicating factor, particularly for finance, is the uncertainty of the actual outcomes for clients and customers. There is an inherent risk in seeking to make gains through investment in financial products and markets. More complicated than blatant misrepresentation and inadequate disclosure as to possible returns are the unrealistic expectations of clients and customers. These are often perpetuated by a general lack of understanding of the complex nature of financial markets, where a single tweet or change to a formula can result in billion-dollar fluctuations, sometimes to the severe disadvantage of investors.

However, the finance sector cannot validly claim financial literacy as the responsibility of the customer or client. There is no doubt that improved financial literacy would result in more-informed decisions and understanding of risk, but for many decades, a range of financial literacy programs has been delivered through schools, governments and various organisations.

The 2014 *Final Report* of the Australian Government Financial System Inquiry warned that 'financial literacy is not a panacea'.[3] It concluded that the sector must take measures to support the fair treatment of customers, in the hope of gaining and keeping their trust and ultimately achieving the status of a profession.

Case Study
Financial Planning in Australia

Much of the dissection of the global financial crisis and ongoing analysis of the financial loss subsequently experienced by customers has focused on the role of the financial planner. There has been a series of cases concerning financial planners who provided inadequate disclosures and unsuitable products, leaving consumers unfairly exposed to financial loss. The deceiving parties have ranged from the suburban planner with a template-form website and domain secured for just 99 cents, to the wealth-management planning arms of globally recognised financial institutions. So while some claim the sector is on a 'journey to professionalism', others claim this is not good enough, and like an impatient child in the back seat on a road trip, they ask, 'Are we there yet?'

The stated objectives of the Future of Financial Advice (FOFA) reforms that became mandatory in Australia in 2013 were to improve the trust and confidence of Australian retail investors in the financial services sector, and to ensure the availability, accessibility and affordability of high-quality financial advice.[4] The objectives were undoubtedly needed and noble. However, implementation has proved more difficult.

The inquiries continued in 2015 with the federal government's consultation on the recommendations of the Parliamentary Joint Committee on Corporations and Financial Services inquiry into proposals to lift the professional, ethical and education standards in the financial services industry.[5] These inquiries have seen the solidification of what it means to establish and transition a segment of the industry to a true profession.

The Australian Bankers' Association, an organisation that provides analysis, advice and advocacy for the banking industry and has twenty-five active member banks, including the largest and most recognised financial institutions in Australia, stated in its comments to the federal government consultation that the banking industry strongly supports raising the professionalism of the financial advice industry. The submission went on to say, 'The Banking industry believes that financial advice should be a profession with higher education, ethical and professional standards'.[6]

Ideas for the setting of educational standards, with minimum-entry qualifications, a registration exam, a graduate professional year and ongoing professional development, have already been well documented. However, the ethical standards and competencies remain less developed and will be subject to a separate standards body. The challenge for this body will be to bring along the range of organisations and individuals in the sector, as well as staying in touch with the community and its desire for the whole process to be fast-tracked.

Robert Brown AM, a chartered accountant with more than thirty years' experience, wrote on Professional Planner that 'It will be the principles adopted in the mandated code of ethics that will determine how directly and how soon the industry completes its hitherto tortuous journey to true professionalism'.[7]

Focus
Individual Purpose

To ponder the question of who it is one works for is an effective way of honestly assessing one's true purpose. For some, perhaps, the answer is simple, but others may have never given the question much consideration. While everyone knows who their employer is, the question of who one really works for, as in whose interests drive the work and win out, can prove a more interesting inquiry and help an individual understand their decisions and actions.

Some work to earn money. For others, work may just be something to do, simply a way of filling in time. Others may work to further their career, to get to the next level with an end goal in mind. Those who work for themselves may be attempting to build something they can leave for their children or sell in the future. Others may work to deliver good service or an experience for customers or clients. There is a range of jobs that help people and attempt to address social challenges, and of course there are people who work for the shareholder, attempting to increase financial returns.

All of these reasons are valid—none is necessarily wrong. However, the decisions and actions of individuals will vary markedly depending on their ultimate motivation and purpose. For those who work for an income to provide for a family or a particular lifestyle, matters at work might appear relatively simple. They may be inclined to just do what is required to get the job done, follow the rules rather than question them, stay in line or even under the radar. The rules and processes that guide behaviour and set an ethical tone may be set somewhere else and not necessarily considered the responsibility of such an individual.

If it's the shareholder who reigns supreme, then it is likely that securing a financial return is what motivates decision and actions. In the finance sector, and particularly in wealth divisions, the customer is often identified as the primary focus, the centre of the business and who is served—it seems obvious, for without the customer, there can be no business. But what happens when a customer's interests are not well served by a decision made in the interest of shareholder returns? An increase in fees, for example, is likely to present a quandary to bank tellers and those in frontline sales roles.

The finance sector was founded upon a social contract with trust at its core. It provides a service that is now an integral component of a civilised society. In fact, the vast majority of the population has little or no choice but to engage in some way with a bank, including compulsory superannuation contributions in Australia. Therefore, an individual working in the finance sector has a broader social obligation and ultimately should consider that their purpose is to work for the good of society, in the public interest.

If an individual was to follow all the rules and abide by all the policies and procedures, they still would be likely to encounter times when they must exercise their own judgement. Remembering this social contract, this broadest of obligations, will inevitably lead to a clearer path for decision-making in such circumstances.

Therefore, for those in finance, the answer to the question 'Who do you work for?' should be simple. They are obliged to work for society. Therefore, having the trust of society is the most important thing of all.

CHANGING EXPECTATIONS OF BUSINESS

The purpose of business is subject to constant inquiry and contention by academics, economists, business leaders and the community. Opinions range from holding that business exists purely to generate profits, to insisting that business has an obligation to contribute to the social good, or should at least be answerable to society.

BUSINESS FOR PROFIT

The theories of American economist Milton Friedman from the early 1970s, particularly his theory that the social responsibility of business is to increase profits,[8] appear to have resonated in the corporate environment. Friedman held that business had just one social responsibility: to use its resources and engage in activities to increase profits. It's important to note that he also emphasised that businesses should stay within 'the rules of the game', in an environment of open and free competition, without deception and fraud. Friedman held that the concept of corporate social responsibility (discussed in detail later in this chapter) undermined the foundations of a free society, and that it was the responsibility of the rest of society to establish the legal and regulatory frameworks whereby an individual in pursuit of their own self-interest could be seen to be led by 'an invisible hand' that promoted an end which was not part of their intention.[9]

Friedman's theories continue to be cited in popular commentary, and his principles can be seen to guide business practices and manage stakeholder expectations. Other objections to the concept of corporate social responsibility include:

- economic objections claiming such practices distort capital allocation
- political objections claiming senior executives should not be allowed to act as unpaid tax collectors and unelected benefactors
- philosophical objections claiming corporations are legal fictions and therefore cannot possess responsibilities.

The acceptance of the premise that business exists to generate profit has been particularly evident through the elevation of the shareholder as the supreme stakeholder. This belief has driven business strategies, investments and staff rewards. Serving the interests of the shareholder has been used as an explanation and justification for decisions and actions both internally and in public forums such as annual general meetings.

Friedman's theories remain the basis for the contention by some organisations and executives that corporate social responsibility is a distraction from their core obligation to act in their shareholders' best interests, which they interpret as seeking maximum financial returns.[10]

ACCOUNTABILITY TO SOCIETY

There are, of course, other schools of thought that believe corporate social responsibility is an inherent obligation of business. Dr Archie Carroll, a business management professor and author, takes a socioeconomic position. He has said that corporations have a responsibility to go beyond profits and protect and improve society, including attempts to fix social problems, particularly those they have had a part in creating; for example, sweatshops, pollution and financial mismanagement.[11]

Others have attempted to promote the business case for corporate social responsibility, arguing that such practices improve trust when it comes to both staff and external stakeholders. They also point to factors such as enhancement of reputation, the strengthening of government relations, and increased joint-venture opportunities.[12] However, the finance sector should be careful in how it perceives and articulates its approach to corporate responsibility. If the driver is seen to be based on self-interest, this may result in cynicism rather than appreciation and trust.

STAKEHOLDER THEORY

As early as the 1980s, shareholder dominance was being questioned by stakeholder theory, as outlined by R Edward Freeman in *Strategic Management: A Stakeholder Approach*.[13] Freeman proposed that the company's aim is to meet the needs of stakeholders; that is, any person who is affected by the decisions made by the company. If this is done, profit will be made. In contrast to business for profit, this theory places emphasis on morals and values in the management of an organisation.

Despite what some might consider the compelling rationale for stakeholder theory, business for profit, with the shareholder as the supreme stakeholder, has largely remained the dominant model of the finance sector. Stakeholder theory appears to have gained only limited mainstream traction. It is more likely to be considered relevant to the areas of corporate social responsibility and responsible investment, as distinct from the core focus—and in turn, purpose—of a business.

CORPORATE SOCIAL RESPONSIBILITY

The corporate social responsibility movement was the evident response of many businesses to the question of their broader responsibility to society. That said, views of corporate social responsibility vary widely.

The International Organization for Standardization's Guidance Standard on Social Responsibility (ISO 26000) states that social responsibility means the responsibility of an organisation for the impacts of its decisions and activities on society and the environment through transparent and ethical behaviour that:

- contributes to sustainable development, including the health and the welfare of society
- takes into account the expectations of stakeholders
- complies with the applicable law and is consistent with international norms of behaviour
- is integrated throughout the organisation and practised in its relationships.[14]

But rather than accept and strategically embed social responsibility throughout an organisation, as defined by the ISO, in the 1980s and 1990s it became common for large financial institutions to establish charitable foundations in order to make donations in support of community programs. In some cases, these foundations were initially based on the interests of the leadership team and staff. Since then, organisations have gradually considered how they might apply the skill sets of their staff to social challenges, with individuals across the finance sector becoming involved in financial literacy programs. This development has seen the rise of volunteer programs for staff, and allowances to incorporate such contributions into the working week.

In Australia in 2015–16, businesses gave a total of A$17.5 billion, as seen in the graph below. The Macquarie Foundation, for example, which was formally established in 1985, provides financial support, volunteering and skills sharing to community organisations around the world each year. The foundation's key objective is to support non-profit organisations within the communities in which Macquarie staff live and work. It focuses on capacity building within the community sector and increasing social and economic mobility. As at 2016, the Macquarie Foundation had contributed in excess of A$300 million to over 3500 community organisations.[15]

The Citi Foundation supports the economic empowerment and financial inclusion of low- and moderate-income people in the communities in which Citigroup companies (including the banking arm) operate. The foundation describes its work to help improve communities as a 'more-than-philanthropy approach', which includes support for program development and skill-based volunteering. In 2004, Citibank

CHARITABLE GIVING BY BUSINESS

Australian business may give money (66% of their total giving), goods (17% of their total giving) or services (18% of their total giving).

In 2015–16, businesses gave $17.5 billion, which comprised

- $7.7 billion in community partnerships
- $6.2 billion in donations
- $3.6 billion in non-commercial sponsorships

Larger businesses tend to give more than small business.

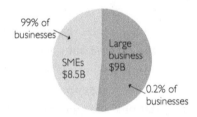

Source: Philanthropy Australia, 'Giving Australia: About the Project', 2017, http://www.philanthropy.org.au/giving-australia

was the first global bank to announce a commitment to meet the growing financial education needs of specific communities—the ten-year commitment was centred on funding of US$200 million.[16]

The philanthropic foundations of some organisations have become increasingly sophisticated in their strategies, seeking to narrow their scope by focusing on a single issue, or selecting a range of issues that they believe will maximise their positive societal impact. However, some have questioned whether businesses can actually balance or counteract their at-times negative impacts with a donation or in-kind contribution to charities or the social sector.

UNDERSTANDING IMPACT THROUGH ENVIRONMENTAL, SOCIAL AND GOVERNANCE ANALYSIS

Environmental, social and governance (ESG) analysis and reporting has recently become more commonplace and integrated across the finance sector. ESG is relevant to both an organisation's own practices and the analysis of investment opportunities.

According to ESG Research Australia, in an investment context, ESG issues are fundamental issues that have the potential to impact a company's financial performance or reputation in a material way, yet are generally not part of traditional fundamental investment analysis. The relevant ESG issues are those that have the potential to materially impact long-term shareholder risks and returns. Examples include the following:

- *environment:* externalities such as pollution and greenhouse gas emissions
- *social:* employee safety issues and community health and wellbeing issues
- *governance:* excessive or poorly structured executive remuneration and board non-independence.

ESG Research Australia believes that traditional financial analysis too often involves too short a time frame, or doesn't include, for example, environmental risks, human resources and social issues.[17]

Financial services organisations are also adopting tools such as those provided by the Global Reporting Initiative, an international independent standards organisation that helps businesses, governments and other organisations understand and communicate their impacts on issues such as climate change, human rights and corruption. They are also committing to initiatives such as the United Nations–backed body Principles for Responsible Investment (PRI). The PRI works to understand the investment implications of ESG factors and to support an international network of investor signatories in incorporating these factors into their investment and ownership decisions. It promotes the fact that it acts in the long-term interests of its signatories, the financial markets and economies in which the signatories operate, and ultimately the environment and society as a whole. The PRI is the world's leading global proponent of responsible investment. As shown in the graph below, by 2016, its signatories numbered over 1500.[18]

Responsible investment is defined as a process that takes account of ESG and ethical issues in the investment process of research, analysis, selection and monitoring of investments. There is a broad array of methods that responsible investors use to manage these non-financial risks, from excluding companies involved in controversial industries, to supporting the most sustainable companies, to a sharp focus on ESG risks, and using ownership to engage with companies.

In Australia and New Zealand, the peak industry body representing responsible and ethical investors is the Responsible Investment

THE RISE OF RESPONSIBLE INVESTMENT

The PRI has grown consistently since it began in 2006.

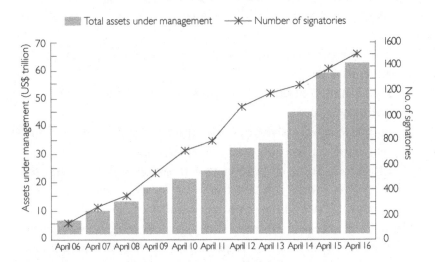

Source: Principles for Responsible Investment, 'About the PRI', 2017,
https://www.unpri.org/about

Association Australasia (RIAA). The RIAA has over 160 members
who manage more than A$1 trillion in assets. These members include
super funds, fund managers, consultants, researchers, brokers, impact
investors, property managers, community banks, community trusts,
religious groups, financial advisers and individuals. The responsible
investment sector constitutes a growing force in the finance and capital
markets of Australasia. In 2016, over 50 per cent of the major super
funds and eight of the top ten fund managers had committed to a more
responsible approach to undertaking investments.[19]

These developments in monitoring, approach and reporting should
result in greater consideration of the broader obligations to society, and
may ultimately lead to a more comprehensive and truer integration of
service to the public within the finance sector.

Case Study
ESG Practices and Measures Questioned in Relation to Tobacco

Engagement is an effective practice used by investment specialists to bring about change in the practices and impact of a business.[20] After undertaking an analysis of ESG factors, an organisation may determine a plan for engagement to encourage better practices, or in the hope that it can increase its performance.

Dr Bronwyn King, founder and CEO of Tobacco Free Portfolios, has said: 'Whilst engagement is a good practice and an example of how the finance sector can be good stewards of capital, there is an exception where engagement has been ineffective—and that is in relation to tobacco'.[21] This position was confirmed by the World Health Organization (WHO) when it issued the following directive: 'The tobacco industry is not and cannot be a partner in effective tobacco control'.[22] According to WHO:

> A large body of evidence demonstrates that tobacco companies use a wide range of tactics to interfere with tobacco control. Such strategies include direct and indirect political lobbying and campaign contributions, financing of research, attempting to affect the course of regulatory and policy machinery, and engaging in social responsibility initiatives as part of public relations campaigns.[23]

Mike Daube AO, professor of health policy at Curtin University in Perth, where he is also the director of the Public Health Advocacy Institute, concurs: 'Where there has been engagement, it has invariably been counterproductive'.[24]

Those in the investment community may feel motivated to encourage better practices by tobacco companies, particularly around youth smoking and child labour in the supply chain. However, despite the much documented and evidenced health impacts of tobacco, it is estimated that in 2012, tobacco companies spent US$9.6 billion—more than US$26 million a day—on advertising and promotional expenditure for cigarettes and smokeless tobacco.[25] According to the US Federal Trade Commission, in 2012, cigarette companies spent 4300 times more money on product marketing and promotions than on youth smoking-prevention advertisements.

A comprehensive report co-released in June 2008 by the US Department of Health and Human Services and the National Cancer Institute, *The Role of the Media in Promoting and Reducing Tobacco Use*, which was based on an exhaustive review of the relevant studies, confirmed that tobacco industry–sponsored youth smoking-prevention programs are generally ineffective at reducing youth smoking and may have caused some youths to start smoking.[26] That same year, a systematic review of mass media campaigns on youth smoking found that tobacco industry–funded youth prevention campaigns had a minimal impact on youth smoking because they avoided the most powerful anti-tobacco themes of health effects and industry manipulation.[27] Yet despite such findings, and the rise of ESG in the finance sector, the inclusion of tobacco in standard financial instruments, and thus investment in tobacco, has continued.

If one were to invest in a socially responsible or sustainable investment option, they would rightly believe that the companies in which they were to become stockholders were in fact sustainable and sought a balance between financial return and social good. If they chose an ethical fund, their expectations would be even higher. Therefore, the inclusion of tobacco companies in, for example, the Dow Jones Sustainability Index may come as a surprise to investors. With tobacco companies now severely limited in relation to advertising and product promotion, their inclusion in globally recognised financial instruments provides a positive promotional opportunity from which they otherwise could not benefit.

It is not uncommon to find tobacco companies, whose cigarettes are responsible for the deaths of two out of three smokers,[28] among the responsible investment and socially responsible investment options offered by mainstream financial institutions. These stocks are included due to the 'best of sector' approach adopted by rating agencies and others in the investment community. 'Best of sector' means that no company is necessarily excluded but is instead judged against its peers. Therefore, at least one tobacco company will receive a triple A rating or three green stars for 'environment', even though non-bio-degradable cigarette butts are the number-one litter item worldwide, fouling waterways and generally proving toxic to the environment.[29]

That a tobacco manufacturer could receive a triple A rating for 'social' seems astounding when the world is on track for one billion deaths this century from tobacco-related illness.[30] Global cooperation is both necessary and evidenced through the WHO Framework Convention on Tobacco Control, the world's first legally binding health treaty, which was established in 2005 and has 180 nation signatories. In addition, in 2015, Bill Gates and Michael Bloomberg established a fund to help poorer nations defend anti-smoking laws designed to protect their people as they implement the treaty.[31]

The inclusion of tobacco, as a matter of course, in indexes and responsible investment options should not remain unquestioned by investors or the finance sector. While the finance system is undoubtedly complex, it is not impossible to track and actively decide investments. In fact, there is growing interest in aligning values with investments. According to the Morgan Stanley Report *Sustainable Signals: The Individual Investor Perspective*, women are nearly twice as likely as men to consider both the potential for returns and the impact of their investments.[32] The US Trust's 2016 annual survey of high-net-worth and ultra-high-net-worth Americans found that two-thirds of millennials wanted to start investing responsibly and were twice as likely to divest from a company because they didn't believe in its work.[33]

In Australia by 2016, due to the advocacy of Dr Bronwyn King through Tobacco Free Portfolios, and the federal government's active role in tobacco control, over thirty-five superannuation funds had implemented completely tobacco-free investment mandates.[34] Also in that year, AXA, one of the world's largest insurers, divested tobacco industry assets valued at 1.8 billion euros.[35] The following year, AMP Capital announced the selling of A$440 million worth of tobacco shares, placing the issue on the mainstream agenda.

Increased transparency, reporting and analysis has helped create a clearer picture of the true impact of a business, from the core product or service to third-party relations. The finance sector, which facilitates much of the investment in business, therefore has an important role to play in both accounting for the true impact of a business in its evaluations, and in setting effective plans for engagement—or in the case of tobacco, not engaging or investing at all.

Interest in responsible and ethical investment is undoubtedly a good development for both the finance sector and the community more broadly. However, there is a need for the finance sector itself to continuously question both the data and the words attached to it, so that investors and the community are not given yet another reason to distrust it.

IMPACT INVESTING

Impact investing refers to investments in companies, organisations and funds with the intention of generating a measurable, beneficial social and/or environmental impact alongside a financial return. It is a form of responsible investment that serves as a guide for various investment strategies, and over the last decade it has been receiving increased attention (see the following graph).

GLOBAL INTEREST IN IMPACT INVESTING

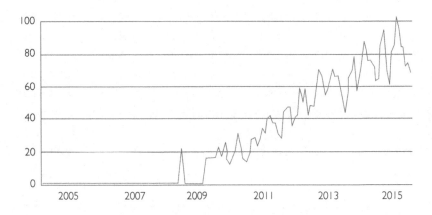

Monthly news headlines featuring 'Impact investing', worldwide

Source: Social Ventures Australia, 'Implications of New Growth Phase in Australian Impact Investing', *SVA Quarterly*, 22 September 2015, http://www.socialventures.com.au/sva-quarterly/implications-of-new-growth-phase-in-australian-impact-investing-2/

Impact Investing Australia, an independent organisation dedicated to creating opportunities for impact investments, profiles STREAT as an example of what can be achieved. STREAT, which was launched in 2009, provides disadvantaged young men and women in Melbourne with the opportunity to build sustainable, long-term careers in hospitality. At-risk young people aged sixteen to twenty-four are offered employment alongside six months of industry training and participation in wellbeing and social support programs. STREAT, one of the first equity-raising social enterprises in Australia, anticipates that its shareholders are set to accrue investment returns of between 7 and 12 per cent per year, generated through the food-service area of the business.[36]

Impact investing is an illustration of the diverse ways in which investment capital can be used to generate positive social and environmental impact alongside financial returns.

SHARED VALUE

Ideas about the purpose of business have continued to evolve, with more recent calls for business to redefine its purpose as the creation of 'shared value', a term introduced by Michael E Porter and Mark R Kramer in their 2011 article 'Creating Shared Value'.[37] Shared value is based on business generating economic value in a way that also produces value for society by addressing societal difficulties and constraints. The peak practice body for shared value in Australasia is the Shared Value Project. It is the regional partner of the Shared Value Initiative, a global community of leaders who find business opportunities in addressing societal challenges.

The Bendigo and Adelaide Bank provides an example of shared value in practice. The 'community bank model' developed by the bank is an alternative approach to providing financial services to rural and smaller metropolitan communities. By supporting their local branch, a community has the opportunity to generate revenue which can be returned to help it develop through community projects, and provide returns to shareholders through dividends—promoting long-term growth.[38]

Shared value obviously presents a challenge to the current approach of many financial services organisations which, despite forays into responsible investment and published ESG positions, seem to be firmly focused on economic value and financial returns.

Case Study
The Slippery Slope of Responsible Investment

Analogies, where one thing is compared with another, are used as a type of shorthand explanation. An analogy is meant to draw a relatable comparison that sums up something so it's easily understood. However, analogies in the context of business can risk being overly simplistic and mistakenly assume a shared understanding.

Some in finance, especially those working in responsible investment and advocating for divestment (where stocks are sold) and exclusions (where a policy prohibits future investment), find that the analogies of 'floodgates' being opened and loss of control on a 'slippery slope' are commonly cited when executives explain their reluctance to consider an issue. After attempting to present clear and confined arguments within a proposed framework, those working in responsible investment are likely to find themselves assuring executives and boards that just by way of considering an investment exclusion for one particular product or service, the floodgates will not open, nor will the business find itself on the way down the dreaded slippery slope.

The 'slippery slope' in particular is now such a common phrase in business that it is cited in meetings and at conferences, on occasion generating no further discussion or inquiry but rather nods of understanding. However, those with decision-making power and influence should instead take the time to reflect on what it is they fear or expect might happen, and consider whether they are in fact practising good decision-making and creating an ethical industry. They could ask themselves, for example, whether they are undertaking a thorough decision-making process that would hold up to public scrutiny.

At the simplest level, there is obviously concern that the consideration (or possible divestment) of one product or service will lead to the forced consideration of other products and services. However, is it good enough for finance executives to avoid addressing the possible, and in some cases known, ethical concerns of investors, advocates and the community? Executives may imagine a line of unruly campaigners, chanting with placards. However, a potentially unmanageable flurry of issues should be met by sound internal processes put in place to both assess and justify investment decisions. A framework can very quickly and easily assist in determining whether investment decisions are principled and match the espoused values and purpose of a product or organisation. Only if the case for divestment is sound will the arguments of an advocate or campaigner hold.

Some executives may lament the extra work that is invariably involved in considering evidence and reassessing an investment decision. This may go some way to explaining the reluctance for not just the movement of funds and stocks but also the reassessment of what might otherwise be considered routine investment decisions, such as investment in standard index funds. The consideration of investment decisions should be a careful practice, and for organisations aspiring to the highest standards, the process will be assisted by an ethical framework. Assessment and reassessment of investment decisions will take time, as the views of others must be heard, the facts considered, and the broader societal context accounted for, with decisions adjusted accordingly.

Where a decision is made to divest or implement an exclusion on the basis of a review, new information or changing social climes, rather than confine the review, it is good practice to consider whether investment in other businesses or sectors should also be reviewed. One could liken the extension of such a review to that of the routine practice of medical professionals. If a doctor were to find evidence of a disease, they would likely extend the area from the original source of complaint, ensuring they had conducted a thorough examination, and enabling them to determine the whole picture of an individual's health. The medical profession rightly refers to its sector as the healthcare sector. Finance might do well to consider itself as having a similar responsibility, but for the wealth care of their clients and customers.

By reframing the situation, investment executives could consider the analysis of investment choices and decisions as an opportunity, perhaps one to create and contribute to a good society. Dealing with issues that aren't necessarily black and white but rather are considered 'grey', where the choices and outcomes are uncertain, can be challenging. However, one could argue this is exactly the reason executives, trustees and directors are appointed— to exercise not just their skills and expertise but also their discretion and good judgement.

Across the finance sector, trustees, directors and senior executives are, on the whole, custodians of the wealth of others. Those that place trust in them should rightfully expect that finance executives will take the time to adequately consider investment positions within the context of society. Finance executives and leaders should be careful not to dismiss such responsibility with an ill-placed analogy. Therefore, it may be time to retire the 'slippery slope' and 'floodgate' references and leave them for a situation where it might be entirely more appropriate, like a farm or a ski field, and not that of investment.

GLOBAL RESPONSIBILITIES—FINANCE AND SUSTAINABLE DEVELOPMENT

With the globalisation of financial markets and the significance of the finance sector to global stability, we have seen the inclusion of the sector in the addressing of global priorities such as poverty alleviation, the assurance of human rights and minimisation of corruption. This extension of responsibility for global issues to the finance sector is evident in such initiatives as the Sustainable Development Goals (SDGs).

The SDGs represent a global consensus on how to achieve a sustainable future through a set of seventeen global goals with targets. The UN General Assembly formally adopted the SDGS in September 2015 and they officially came into force on 1 January 2016. All countries are expected to consider the SDGs when preparing plans and policies. And the international community, including the UN, the World Bank and regional development banks, as well as public and private donors, is expected to assist governments to reach the SDGs.

In October 2016, UN secretary-general Ban Ki-moon announced the launch of a platform designed to scale innovative finance solutions to support achievement of the SDGs. The launch was attended not only by high-level officials from various ministries of finance and foreign affairs, but also by the leaders of major global financial institutions. The secretary-general, addressing the high-level finance gathering, said:

> This global initiative can support the identification and piloting of innovative finance instruments that can drive investment and support well thought-out SDG interventions. As well as launching innovative financing solutions, the Platform would engage key Development actors, including Governments, civil society, philanthropic organizations, entrepreneurs, institutional investors, banks, project developers and development finance institutions.[39]

In the Australian context, in 2016, then Australian Human Rights Commission president Gillian Triggs declared, 'It is the hope of the Australian Human Rights Commission to work much more closely with the investment community'. Triggs believed that major institutional investors, such as superannuation funds, 'have the power in their hands' to encourage the companies they invest in to adhere to the UN's guiding principles on human rights. However, she highlighted the need for development and a change of approach, as according to Triggs, business practices in Australia have not been looked at 'through the prism of international human rights law'.[40]

ADJUSTING MEASURES OF SUCCESS
TENDENCY TO MEASUREMENT

By its very nature—involving money—the finance industry and its performance is susceptible to quantitative analysis and measurement. Historically, the success of the industry and its people has been judged by profits. Increasingly, however, society has sought to judge the finance industry's performance and role according to broader criteria, such as its social and environmental impact and ethical conduct. At times, even the social licence to operate has been called into question.

As the sector largely draws people from fields of study such as economics, accounting and finance, it naturally tends to preference measurement and is well accustomed to a reliance on assumptions in the provision of certainty. Perhaps, given the academic training and developed skill sets of the majority of those in the sector, it is not particularly surprising that while economic theories have been subject to waves of acceptance, with assumptions periodically questioned, measurable outcomes can be seen to dominate in the shaping of everything from investment decisions to the promotion and remuneration of staff. Dr Simon Longstaff of The Ethics Centre identifies the trend of measurement as reflective of 'people attempting to create certainty in what is essentially an uncertain world'. It is interesting, then, to consider how the industry might successfully transition to professionalisation with the key pillars of ethics and public service, which are open to subjective interpretation, subject to ongoing change, and ultimately resistant to measurement.

ATTEMPTS TO ADDRESS ETHICS

Statements championing values such as integrity, honesty and care, among others, have been commonplace across the finance sector for decades and are referenced by finance leaders when explaining the ethics of their organisations. Disappointingly, companies subject to both small- and large-scale cases of fraud and public ethical lapses have had such values statements in place, indicating the difficulty in truly motivating and inspiring staff to shape their decisions and behaviours in accordance with espoused organisational values. In 2016, for example, Wells Fargo employees created millions of unauthorised bank and credit card accounts without customers knowing, earning the bank unwarranted fees and boosting sales figures.[41] This happened despite 'ethics' being one of the organisation's five espoused values.

As a US-based international banking and financial services holding company, Wells Fargo described its approach to ethics as follows: 'We strive to be recognised by our stakeholders as setting the standard among the world's great companies for integrity and principled performance. This is more than just doing the right thing. We also have to do it in the right way'.[42] With 5300 Wells Fargo employees identified as being involved in the accounts scandal, with their employment subsequently terminated, it's clear that the organisational values were not properly integrated across the business.

This is not a new phenomenon. Enron, an American energy, commodities and services company once lauded by Fortune as 'America's

Most Innovative Company', went bankrupt in 2001 as a result of systemic accounting fraud despite having considered itself a 'Global Corporate Citizen' with the espoused values of respect, integrity, communication and excellence.[43]

It is not just a case of fraud in America. In 2016, the Commonwealth Bank of Australia's insurance arm, CommInsure, was subject to investigation and the finding that customer assessments had been altered to avoid payouts, that payouts to terminally ill customers were delayed, and other claims were not honoured.[44] This followed the financial planning scandal of 2008, where a Senate inquiry found forgery and dishonest concealment of material facts at Commonwealth Financial Planning Limited, part of the Commonwealth Bank of Australia Group.[45] In 2016, CommInsure's board chairman, Geoff Austin, claimed, 'The concerns raised in the recent cases reported are not a reflection of the values of our people or our business'. This came after the 2015 annual general meeting where Commonwealth Bank chairman David Turner said, 'We think we will be the ethical bank, the bank others look up to for honesty, transparency, decency, good management, openness. That is exactly where we are trying to go'.[46] This comment is clearly a statement of intention. At the same meeting, the bank's CEO, Ian Narev, said, 'Trust is at the heart of banking. It's not good enough if trust or good ethics exist in the vast majority of the organisation. You've got to do your best to get it right across the organisation'.

The Australian Prudential Regulatory Authority (APRA), in its October 2016 Information Paper 'Risk Culture', stated that 'What an institution really values and sees as important will be evidenced by the behaviours of its staff'. APRA also acknowledged the practical difficulties involved in making organisation-wide values meaningful as behavioural drivers.[47]

It is evident that values statements and management intention are not enough to encourage and guide ethical behaviour in the hope of gaining trust. Instead, they are merely components of a broader approach. As with training and self-regulation, values statements and management declarations are easier to design and launch than used to truly instil a sense of purpose in staff that has service to society at its core.

Following the global financial crisis, the finance sector has seen the wider adoption of ethics training modules within organisations. Even as early as the mid-1990s, these programs had become the norm at Fortune 1000 companies. However, a study in the *Journal of Business Ethics* found that while there had been a high degree of corporate adoption of ethics policies, there was wide variability in the extent to which the policies were implemented by various supporting structures and managerial activities. The authors of the study concluded that, in effect, the vast majority of organisations had committed to the low-cost, possibly symbolic side of ethics management—for example, through the adoption of ethics codes and policies—but that organisations differed substantially in their efforts to see that those policies or codes were actually put into practice.[48]

In Australia in 2015, the Ethical Professional Program was announced as an initiative of The Ethics Centre, an independent not-for-profit organisation, in collaboration with a range of financial services organisations, with its development overseen by APRA, ASIC, the Association of Financial Advisers, Financial Planning Association, SMSF Association, Financial Services Council and the Australian Bankers' Association. The program had the declared aim of equipping people working across the financial advice sector with the knowledge and skills necessary to make ethically sound decisions. John Neil, co-head of advice and education at The Ethics Centre, emphasised that the 'Ethical Professional Program draws on contemporary research in ethics and neuroscience to support the understanding of how ethics relates to the day-to-day work of people employed across the industry'.[49]

However, while there is some evidence that ethics training programs have an impact,[50] there is little academic literature analysing more recent efforts. Ethics training therefore remains just one component of the attempt to professionalise the finance sector and restore trust.

CALLS FOR A NEW APPROACH

Leaders in Australia, like others across the globe, have called for a focus on culture and ethics in response to the responsibilities and risks of the finance sector. National Australia Bank chairman Dr Ken Henry said in April 2016:

> Corporate leaders have responsibility for the culture of organisations and they all kind of know it, but they're struggling with how to do it and how to be effective ... Boards should talk to senior management.

Whatever opportunities they have, they should talk to staff about the values of the organisation.[51]

Dr Henry's statements followed comments made by Glenn Stevens, former governor of the Reserve Bank of Australia, at the 2015 *Australian Financial Review* Banking and Wealth Summit:

> The final issue is misconduct. This has loomed larger for longer in many jurisdictions than we would have thought likely a few years ago. Investigations and prosecutions for alleged past misconduct are ongoing. It seems our own country has not been entirely immune from some of this. Without in any way wanting to pass judgement on any particular case, root causes seem to include distorted incentives coupled with an erosion of a culture that placed great store on acting in a trustworthy way.
>
> Finance depends on trust. In fact, in the end, it can depend on little else. Where trust has been damaged, repair has to be made.
>
> In the end, though, you can't legislate for culture or character. Culture has to be nurtured, which is not a costless exercise. Character has to be developed and exemplified in behaviour. For all of us in the financial services and official sectors, this is a never-ending task.

In April 2016, ASIC chairman Greg Medcraft, in conversation with Dr Simon Longstaff, discussed the limits of regulation in relation to culture: 'Culture needs to be determined by leadership because you can't regulate culture ... that's up to the company themselves'.[52] Medcraft continued with this theme in a speech at the launch of the Governance Institute of Australia's inaugural Ethics Index in July 2016:

> ASIC is interested in corporate culture, because culture is a driver of conduct. And a poor corporate culture can be a driver of misconduct. Conversely, a good corporate culture can be a driver of best practice, or ethical conduct. Ethical conduct can help organisations move beyond minimum standards and tick-a-box compliance practices, to best practice standards and compliance practices that protect stakeholders and which are commercially valuable.

The integrity of Australia's financial markets is critical to ensuring the trust and confidence of customers and the community. It is clear that concern for investors and consumers is central to the focus on culture and ethics within financial services, and some would say this is all long overdue. Still, regulators and organisations are turning to culture and risk conduct as priority areas of focus. Supervisors and bank leaders have shown increased concern that the root cause of conduct and other issues is a more fundamental problem requiring long-term culture change.[53]

As work cultures within the finance sector are analysed and monitored, organisations will no doubt be challenged by the difficulties involved in definitively measuring culture. Instead, they must become accustomed to 'indicators' of ethical cultures, and accept that ensuring the ethics and good work cultures of the sector will be a complex and ongoing task.[54]

Focus

Incentives and the Finance Sector

Concern regarding the ethics of remuneration practices in the finance sector has been evident for some time, with ongoing public calls for formal reviews of incentive schemes. The concerns tend to focus on incentives that have encouraged excessive risk-taking and resulted in individuals putting the interests of themselves and their organisation over all others, often to the detriment of the customer. It is evident that addressing such concerns will be crucial to the finance sector gaining trust and professional standing.

Headlines such as 'Banks Are to Blame for the Public Backlash',[55] 'Big Bonuses Breed Toxic Culture'[56] and 'Bank Salaries Are Ridiculous'[57] indicate the prevailing sentiment among the media and the community. This was confirmed by the 2016 report *Time to Listen*, released by the UK arm of professional services company PwC.[58] It asserted that two-thirds of the UK's population thought top executive salaries were too high, and over half thought it was a big problem. Most people thought a CEO should earn no more than twenty times the average earnings, compared with typical pay ratios in the FTSE 100 of over 150 times. Eighty-seven per cent of the public believed something must be done about this.

The Rise of CEO Salaries

There appears to be disagreement as to whether incentives are beneficial or detrimental to organisations. It is important to note that incentive payments were not always common to financial services. Harrison Young, a director of the Commonwealth Bank, said at the 2015 *Australian Financial Review* Banking and Wealth Summit that 'the men who taught me banking in the early 70s were sceptical about money, full stop. So long as your salary puts dinner on the table, they would tell you, the right reward for bankers is the regard of their peers'[59] The Productivity Commission reported that until the mid-1990s, the norm in Australia was for executives to be paid a fixed salary plus some allowances and benefits.[60]

Some claim the norm changed in 1993 when Westpac, one of the four major banks in Australia, was in a state of crisis and it was decided to recruit an American to the position of CEO.[61] In the United States at that time, it was already commonplace for those in senior positions to be remunerated far above the salary of the average employee. As a result, Robert Joss, former vice chairman of Wells Fargo, was offered the Westpac position in line with the compensation packages in his home country. Joss was granted a base salary of A\$1.9 million with A\$6.9 million in share options—by way of comparison, the CEO of the Commonwealth Bank was being paid around A\$500 000.[62]

In their recent book *Stop Paying Executives for Performance*, Dan Cable, professor of organisational behaviour at London Business School, and Freek Vermeulen, associate professor of strategic and international management at the London Business School, in arguing that performance incentives should be abolished, set out five reasons why executives should only be paid a fixed salary:

1. Performance incentives really only work for jobs involving routine tasks.
2. Fixating on performance can weaken it, when focusing on learning can actually improve outcomes.
3. Intrinsic motivation crowds out extrinsic motivation.
4. Contingent pay leads to 'cooking the books', causing people to distort the truth regarding goal attainment.
5. All measurement systems are flawed. It is simply not possible to precisely measure someone's actual performance, given that it consists of many different stakeholders' interests, tangible and tacit resources, and short- and long-term effects.[63]

When considering the ethics of incentives and compensation packages, inequity and fairness are commonly discussed. CEO and senior executive pay across the corporate sector has steadily risen over the years, and it is not uncommon for a banking executive to be paid more than a doctor or a judge.

In 2015, the ratio between the average American CEO pay and worker pay was 303:1.[64] In Australia in 2014, the ratio was 93:1.[65] While there have been calls for public disclosure of such ratios, and even limits to the disparity, such changes have yet to be adopted widely across the finance sector, or the corporate community in general.

In cases like that of Joss in the early 1990s, the remuneration package was seen as necessary to attract the right 'talent' to the position. The individual was seen to be compensated for taking a difficult or risky job, or relocating to an unfamiliar market. However, Jeffrey Moriarty, an associate professor of philosophy at Bentley University in Massachusetts, whose work focuses on business ethics, highlighted that this should no longer be the case, as there is no shortage of the talented and dedicated people that make up a global workforce. He concluded that executives were being paid more than what was necessary to attract talent.[66]

There is another ethical aspect to this beyond issues of inequity and fairness. For publicly listed banks and financial institutions, the more money that is spent on executive remuneration, the less there is to pay dividends to the shareholders or reinvest in the organisation.

Issues of inequity and fairness, and discussions of the character traits that incentive schemes should encourage, continue to be discussed and debated across the finance sector. The PWC report *Time to Listen* warned, 'We need to find a way to respond to public concerns about executive pay, or matters will be taken out of our hands'. It would seem that it is time for finance leaders to not just listen but to act.[67]

CONCLUSION

We've moved a long way from the brass shingle that signalled a professional was fit to provide their services to organisations with an online presence only, no shopfront at all. In fact, many in financial services will have no physical—or indeed any—contact with a customer. Without the sense of responsibility and accountability that develops naturally when one engages directly in a relationship, it is imperative that individuals in financial services are driven by the greater good of public service.

The challenge for the finance sector is to get the entire industry to think this way. The challenge for individuals already in the sector, and committed to public service, is to bring their colleagues and team members along with them. Young people, many of whom have been

educated in a different manner to their seniors through the incorpo-
ration of ethics in undergraduate programs, and who may have had a
different sense of purpose instilled in them, will likely play a crucial role
in the finance sector's journey to professionalism.

Service to the public, or at least an acknowledgement of the obligation to be accountable to society, may become an inevitable outcome
as organisations move towards the true integration of factors relating
to the environment, social impact and governance, and as interest in
responsible investment grows. However, the finance sector must remain
aware that, for some, this outcome will have been driven by competition and market demand rather than the sense of service that is the
mark of a true profession.

Some may claim this doesn't matter, as the outcome will be achieved.
Yet, if a sense of service is not in operation above all other drivers,
then the professional will remain susceptible to conflicting priorities
and inconsistent practices as they respond to market developments and
clients' wants rather than ethical principles.

It is also evident that executive pay and incentive schemes have
contributed to what the sector refers to as a 'trust gap',[68] in that the
trust and confidence of the public is not at the level the leaders of the
sector would like it to be, or believe it should be. Historical measures
of success related to profits and market share are no longer considered
enough, or appropriate. While it remains a challenge for finance organisations and executives to both understand and satisfy society's ethical
expectations, it would appear the ongoing social licence to operate will
depend upon it.

3

SOMETHING SO STRONG
Foundations of Trust
Clare Payne

THE ROLES AND LIMITS OF REGULATION AND LEGISLATION

Initially in response to the global financial crisis, there was a proliferation of prescriptive legislation, regulation and compliance measures. However, the right balance between laws, regulation and trust in the sector in self-regulating is still being determined. It would appear the sector has some way to go in assuring governments, regulators and the public that it can be trusted to do what is right, regardless of the regulatory and legal minimums.

The decades-long swelling of staff in both traditional and new banking activities has been met by the creation of many more risk and compliance roles in an attempt to implement regulatory requirements while simultaneously anticipating further developments. At J.P.Morgan, the number of staff working in compliance and regulation had grown to 43 000 by 2016, compared with 23 000 in 2011. The American Bankers Association estimated that, in 2013, the top six banks (ranked by assets) spent US$70 billion on compliance, nearly double that of the year prior.[1] In 2014, the four major Australian banks collectively spent A$1.67 billion on implementation costs relating to the US Foreign Account Tax Compliance Act, the FOFA reforms, anti-money laundering practices, privacy (including credit reporting), e-payments, the Financial Claims Scheme, over-the-counter derivative reforms, and the *National Consumer Credit Protection Act 2009*.[2]

Deloitte's 2014 *Global Risk Management Survey*, subtitled *Operating in the New Normal: Increased Regulation and Heightened Expectations*, concluded that

> the focus of regulators on such issues as capital adequacy, liquidity, operational risk, governance, and culture is driving change throughout the financial industry. The impacts have been widespread as new requirements continue to be proposed by regulators around the world, even as the final rules to implement existing laws are still being written. Complying with multiple, sometimes conflicting, regulatory requirements implemented by different regulatory authorities poses a significant challenge for global financial institutions.[3]

In 2015, in an address at the Federal Reserve Bank of New York, Christine Lagarde, managing director of the International Monetary Fund (IMF), highlighted as good news the financial reform agenda that has continued since the global financial crisis. Lagarde focused on the importance of reforming compensation and governance structures to reduce excessive risk-taking.[4]

It must be acknowledged, however, that there is often tension between regulation and the finance sector, with claims that the former can restrict and stifle the way in which the latter does business. When faced with new or restrictive regulations, finance organisations have been known to circumvent them by relisting and conducting equity capital raising in other locations where they can operate under less sophisticated and far-reaching regulatory regimes. Some claim the continued regulatory reaction to the global financial crisis and ongoing incidences of poor behaviour in financial services have actually served to exacerbate the problem by creating a risk-management culture rather than an ethics-based culture.

Importantly, it is evident that, rather than view regulatory measures as a minimum baseline for governance, some in the finance sector view compliance with corporate governance guidelines as the ultimate ethical goal. While regulation of the finance sector by formal regulatory mechanisms—both government and self-regulation—is essential, it is not enough. Regulation cannot address every possibility and every eventuality of human behaviour, particularly considering the complexity of finance and global markets. Some hold that where there is opportunity, there will be attempts to finance it.

In addition, we have seen the proliferation of financial products that are increasingly difficult to understand, particularly in new markets where financial institutions trade in newly created financial instruments and products. These markets and financial products thus pose an exceptionally difficult challenge for lawmakers and regulators, who can find it hard to keep up with rapid financial innovation. While laws provide an essential framework within which organisations can compete and cooperate, it is important to note that they are not removed from society but rather are a reflection of society's moral and ethical standards.

As with the proliferation of regulation in finance, there has also been a series of legislative amendments and new laws around the world, the best-known being the 2002 US Sarbanes-Oxley Act. The United Kingdom created a Combined Code on Corporate Governance, and in 2013 established the Financial Conduct Authority. Australia responded by implementing amendments to the *Corporate Law Economic Reform Program Act 2004* and various corporate governance codes. There has been an evident increase in the complexity of legislation, particularly in the Australian *Corporations Act*, as shown below.

Laws play an important role in acting as a deterrent, as well as setting minimum standards. However, as with regulation, there are limits to the effectiveness of the law. Legislation tends to significantly lag developments and practices. In addition, some people claim that laws do not go far enough, with financial service providers receiving fines that don't necessarily serve to discourage or change behaviours. In 2016, ASIC chairman Greg Medcraft claimed that penalties for bad behaviour among bankers were not strong enough to deter individuals from ripping off customers.[5]

It is estimated that in the six years prior to 2015, fines levied on large banks in the United States and Europe amounted to US$230 billion.[6] The IMF warned that such sanctions directed at financial institutions

INCREASE IN COMPLEXITY OF THE AUSTRALIAN
CORPORATIONS ACT FROM 1981 TO 2015

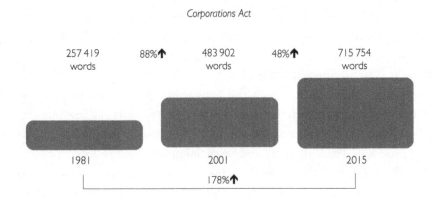

Corporations Act

| 257 419 words | 88%↑ | 483 902 words | 48%↑ | 715 754 words |

| 1981 | 2001 | 2015 |

178%↑

Source: Social Ventures Australia, 'Implications of New Growth Phase in Australian Impact Investing', *SVA Quarterly*, 22 September 2015, http://www.socialventures.com.au/ sva-quarterly/implications-of-new-growth-phase-in-australian-impact-investing-2/

have come to be perceived as a cost of doing business. Hence, the organisation's support for the strengthening of personal accountability through criminal and civil liability.

One of the key objectives of financial regulation is to promote safe and sound risk-taking decisions, and such legal and regulatory frameworks will play an important part in driving cultural change within the finance sector. However, it is generally understood that regulation is only as good as its implementation by the industry and its enforcement by the supervisor. As ethics is prioritised by the finance sector, its leaders must remain aware that excessive reliance on regulation and supervision can risk allowing people to feel that as long as they are complying and meeting minimum standards, then they are acting ethically, which, as Christine Lagarde concluded in her 2015 speech to the Federal Reserve Bank of New York, 'is not always the case'.[7]

The implementation of legislation and regulations, in both letter and spirit, remains a challenge for the finance sector. In her speech, Lagarde also outlined a three-pillar framework for instilling ethical behaviour in financial services:

1. regulation
2. governance
3. the individual.

Lagarde went on to say, 'The individual is the third pillar, without which there can be no equilibrium'. She concluded: 'The appropriate regulatory and governance framework must be in place to support the ethics of behaviour and individuals. Yet the opposite is also true. Without individual integrity, even the best regulatory and governance structures can be gamed'.

GOOD GOVERNANCE

The Organisation for Economic Co-operation and Development defines corporate governance as a set of relationships between a company's management, its board, shareholders and other stakeholders.[8] Corporate governance provides the structure through which the objectives of the company are set, and the means by which attaining those objectives and monitoring performance are determined. In the 2010 publication *Enhancing Corporate Governance for Banking Organisations*, the Basel Committee on Banking Supervision set out the arguments as to why corporate governance is of greater importance to financial services than to other sectors and companies.[9] The following points were highlighted:

- the crucial role of financial intermediation by banks in the economy
- the need to safeguard depositors' funds
- the potential impacts and ramifications of ineffective corporate governance.

The committee stated that effective corporate governance practices, on both a system-wide and individual-organisation basis, are essential to achieving and maintaining public trust and confidence in the banking system, which in turn are critical to the proper functioning of the banking and finance sectors and the economy as a whole.

Discussions of governance in Australia have increasingly focused on the responsibilities of the board of directors. The Australian Institute of Company Directors (AICD) manages the Governance Leadership Centre, a think tank that provides perspectives on governance, focusing on the link with business performance. The AICD also promotes board diversity for governance and performance.

John Laker, in his 2005 address *Corporate Governance in Financial Institutions* as APRA chairman, stated clearly the important role of the company board:

> It is the board that should set the strategic direction of the institution and approve and review significant policies. It is the board that should determine the institution's tolerance for risk, approve its risk management strategy and policies, and ensure that management is monitoring the effectiveness of risk controls. It is the audit or risk committee of the board that should satisfy itself that all material risks are identified, that appropriate risk management systems are in place, and that the monitoring and audit process highlight any significant issues or weaknesses. It is the board that should ensure that the institution maintains capital resources commensurate with the level and type of risk exposure. And it is the board which should take the lead in establishing the culture and ethical values of the institution, setting the tone at the top.[10]

Regulators have steadily increased their level of engagement with boards, seeking a better understanding of the working relationships between the board, the CEO and executives so they can properly assess the effectiveness of governance arrangements. In addition, board composition is an area of continuing inquiry as chairs and organisations seek the right combination of independence and experience to create an effective board dynamic. This dynamic, being the way members of the board work with each other as well as with the CEO, senior management and other stakeholders, is currently an area of focus and commentary.[11]

One may question how a director can be confident that they have enough information and insight to make the informed decisions for which they will be held accountable. The AICD, along with a variety of consultants and advisers, works to educate directors, highlighting not just the processes and structures that should be in place in the organisations in which they hold positions, but also giving guidance as to the questions they should be asking.[12] Good decision-making frameworks, such as those outlined in Chapter 7, apply equally to directors as to other individuals working within the finance sector; recent cases have highlighted that it is the process of inquiry by directors that matters.[13]

Also see Chapter 4, where the concept of fiduciary duty is explored in detail.

Organisations commonly have many internal governance policies and processes that are designed to support individuals, including:

- regular reporting and monitoring, in both formal reports and at meetings
- training and professional development, including ethics, diversity and compliance
- whistleblowing, including hotlines and 'speak-up' programs
- values statements, codes of conduct and codes of ethics.

Many individuals working in the finance sector will have little direct interaction with regulators, the board of the organisation that employs them, or even the senior executive team. Therefore, these governance policies and processes are essential in supporting individuals to make good decisions and develop as ethical leaders.

INDIVIDUAL ACCOUNTABILITY AND SELF-REGULATION

Across the finance sector globally, there have been increasing calls—and a subsequent focus on—the accountability of individuals for the impacts of their decisions and behaviours. This is in contrast to the historical approach of organisations being held accountable for the actions of their staff. This change is being called for by regulators, customers and the community more broadly, all of whom wish to see individuals held accountable for the impact and losses experienced by customers as a result of poor financial advice, excessive risk-taking, and products that have operated unethically. Regulators are responding by taking steps to hold individuals accountable for their actions. This has resulted in people being subject to not just disciplinary procedures within an organisational setting, but also prosecution in courts that can lead to fines, criminal or civil liability, and professional disbarment.

The IMF's Christine Lagarde publicly approved of this strengthening of personal accountability, believing it will provide the right set of incentives for ethical behaviour. In November 2015, in an address at the Federal Reserve Bank of New York, Lagarde called for a culture of greater virtue and integrity at the individual level in financial services.

She specifically stated that cultural change within the sector should involve appealing to the 'moral compass' of individuals.

A number of industry and professional associations provide support, education and professional development for individuals working in the finance sector. These associations are often focused on a distinct segment of the sector, such as accountants, actuaries or analysts. Such associations have an important self-regulatory role in setting and promoting professionalism. Increasingly, they are also focusing on ethics and conduct, and considering their role in enhancing and ensuring trust in the finance sector. Many also promote codes covering conduct and ethics, and provide training on ethics, leadership and governance.

Active associations in financial services in Australia include the following:

- Accounting and Finance Association of Australia and New Zealand (AFAANZ)
- Actuaries Institute
- Association of Financial Advisers (AFA)
- Association of Super Funds of Australia (ASFA)
- Australian Bankers Association (ABA)
- Australian Council of Superannuation Investors (ACSI)
- Australian Finance Conference (AFC)
- Australian Financial Markets Association (AFMA)
- Australian Institute of Superannuation Trustees (AIST)
- Australian Securitisation Forum (ASF)
- Certified Practising Accountants (CPA) Australia
- Chartered Accountants ANZ (CA ANZ)
- Chartered Financial Analyst (CFA) Institute
- Customer Owned Banking Association (COBA)
- Finance Brokers Association of Australia Limited (FBAA)
- Financial Management Association of Australia (FMAA)
- Financial Planning Association of Australia (FPA)
- Financial Services Council (FSC)
- Financial Services Institute of Australasia (FINSIA)
- Fund Executives Association Limited (FEAL)
- Investment Management Consultants Association (IMCA)
- Mortgage and Finance Association of Australia (MFAA)
- Responsible Investment Association Australasia (RIAA)

- Self Managed Super Fund (SMSF) Association
- Women in Banking and Finance (WIBF).

These associations undoubtedly play an important role in promoting high ethical standards, and holding their members to them. Such associations are increasingly pointed to by the finance sector as an assurance they can engage in self-regulation.

Chartered Accountants ANZ, for example, has been active in championing and addressing ethics both within its member base and across the sector more broadly. In 2016, as part of its *future[inc]: Perspectives on Prosperity* series, the association commissioned and launched the publication *A Question of Ethics: Navigating Ethical Failure in the Banking and Financial Services Industry*. The paper proposed a range of what were termed 'culture-shaping' interventions, designed to improve ethical behaviour in the banking and financial services sector. The suggested interventions included:

- harnessing data analytics to measure and reward non-financial performance
- engaging in conscious, principled reasoning—focusing on explicitly stated non-negotiable principles instead of cost–benefit calculations
- reducing the risk of insularity and groupthink by encouraging a diverse range of views, from team to board level
- making ethics a part of everyday conversation—an inquiry into how practices such as short conversations about ethical issues at the beginning of meetings, to create an 'ethical frame' and decision-making frameworks, can help individuals prioritise ethics.[14]

It is interesting to note the stated intention of Chartered Accountants ANZ in specifically addressing ethics in banking and financial services. The recommendations as outlined in *A Question of Ethics* were designed to 'promote debate amongst key industry stakeholders' with the specific intention of 'challenging organisations to develop comprehensive, evidence-based ethics programs that recognise the sector's unique dynamics and offer a realistic opportunity for genuine cultural change'.

Accountants, who are obliged to belong to such an association in order to promote themselves as a practising accountant, could be seen as representing one of the most professionalised sections of the finance

sector. Indeed, the proposed measures to professionalise financial planning and advice are well established in accounting, and accountants
may therefore be justified in seeing themselves as distinct from other
parts of the sector—although accounting too has been susceptible to
fraud and ethical lapses, highlighting the importance of the constant
reinforcement of ethical standards.

Case Study
Self-Regulation through The Banking and Finance Oath

In 2010, a group of like-minded leaders in the banking and finance industry
in Australia, with the support of The Ethics Centre, decided to explore the
possibility of creating an initiative that would reassert the ethical foundation
of the industry as a whole. Given the global scope of the industry, and the
diversity of the businesses within it, it was agreed that a credible initiative that
transcended membership of any particular corporation or jurisdiction was
required. It was this requirement that led to the development of The Banking
and Finance Oath, commonly referred to as The BFO.

The BFO is a set of professional principles freely entered into by individuals who choose to be accountable to each other for upholding them. The
model was loosely based on, first, the Hippocratic oath that binds physicians
personally, irrespective of where they work, and second, the ethical code that
bound the early Enlightenment scientists into a virtual 'commonwealth' that
allowed them to work collaboratively, to a common set of standards, despite
being separated.

The vision of The BFO is a banking and finance industry that meets the
community's needs and has its full confidence. Former APRA chairman John
Laker said:

> The BFO is founded on a shared belief in the inherent good of the banking
> and finance industry, and is an effort to reassert the ethical foundation of
> the industry by providing a simple set of tenets that can promote personal
> accountability and can encourage discussions, in the workplace and outside,
> that involve ethics, integrity and trust.[15]

Through volunteering to take the oath and being accountable at the
individual level, the directors who guide the initiative intend to establish a
foundation of trust across the sector, impacting internal cultures and in turn
better serving customers and upholding the spirit of service to the public.

Signatories are not invested with any special degree of virtue; rather, the whole initiative is based on a framework of interpersonal accountability and the provision of a supportive environment that prompts personal reflection about practices where good people find themselves doing bad things simply because 'that's the way it has always been done' or because 'everybody does it that way'.

Individuals become signatories by agreeing to adopt each principle of the oath online at http://www.thebfo.org. The wording of the oath is as follows:

Trust is the foundation of my profession.

I will serve in good faith.

I will compete with honour.

I will pursue my ends with ethical restraint.

I will help create a sustainable future.

I will help create a more just society.

I will speak out against wrongdoing and support others who do the same.

I will accept responsibility for my actions.

In these and all other matters;

My word is my bond.[16]

The BFO board believes that regulation will only be truly effective when a common ethical foundation, such as that provided by The BFO, is widely adopted by individuals rather than organisations. The ideal for The BFO is an industry where signatories to the oath can look beyond their corporation and find 'like-minded individuals' with an ethical commitment held in common.

Ultimately, The BFO is a tool that can help put greater emphasis on individual accountability for decision-making. The success of the initiative is still perceived by many as an ambitious goal, but its founders believe it can play an important role in shaping the industry and rebuilding its relationship with society.

Focus
Values Alignment

Some individuals may not feel any particular alignment between their personal values and their professional life. A telecommunications engineer who believes in the benefit of delivering advanced technology to emerging nations may work as an analyst scoping online casino deals for an investment bank. An architect with a PhD in sustainable housing for communities affected by natural disasters may work for a large construction company erecting towering apartment blocks in Dubai, and a public relations manager whose father died of lung cancer may find herself working for a beverage company owned by a tobacco company. There are many examples of people whose professional careers, whose application of their given talents or skills, actually conflicts with their personal values and interests.

However, perhaps the more interesting phenomenon is that this incongruence may not be questioned, by the individual or others. People do not necessarily make the connection between what they do and the subsequent effect on society. This often occurs because of complex corporate structures that obscure the direct role and impact of individuals.

Some may see themselves as merely playing a role in the workplace, as if an actor, with little accountability or control over the direction the company is taking, or the script it has written. They just perform tasks, often in teams, and don't question how this fits in with and shapes the bigger picture. If questioned, of course, there are various justifications they may adopt in an attempt to explain the misalignment of their personal values with their professional life. Rationales may be proposed such as, 'Well, it's legal. There's regulation about how much a gaming company can take from a machine'. Or: 'The government gives the contracts to the construction companies. I don't decide'. Or: 'It's the CEO and management that make the decisions, not me'. All these justifications declare that accountability for the moral and ethical aspects of business, and the individual's work, ultimately rests with someone else.

Then there are those who have acknowledged the incongruence at a personal level, and they have a plan. They may say, 'I'm only doing this for a few years. Then I want to go work for Médicins sans Frontières'. Or: 'We're thinking of setting up a reading group for kids, in our spare time'. There is a sense that what they are doing now can be balanced out by some good they will do later.

There are also many personal factors that an individual may consider beyond their control and that have led them to hold a conflict of values, such as, 'It's the only big employer in my area', or 'I have a mortgage and kids. I have to run a household'. Other individuals may point to the philanthropic work of their organisation, or their personal involvement in various charitable organisations and not-for-profits. Again, there is the sense that the impact of their work can somehow be balanced out.

But all of these justifications demonstrate a lack of personal accountability in the present, and for some, a shunning of their conscience. Despite the attribution of human qualities to corporations, they clearly lack a conscience, or human emotions such as guilt, worry or sadness. The moral and ethical mindset of an organisation is instead made up of the individuals who operate within it and represent it publicly. Therefore, each individual has a role to play in setting and shaping an ethical tone.

As individuals in the finance sector consider their responsibilities and accept personal accountability for their decisions, the alignment of personal and professional values can act to simplify decision-making and lead to a deeper understanding of the impact of not just the individual, but also the finance sector.

CONCLUSION

The finance sector needs to recognise the shortcomings of legislation and regulation, and acknowledge the complex grey areas where individuals have to make difficult decisions that have ethical dimensions. A comprehensive, constantly developing and responsive regulatory and legislative system does need to be part of corporate governance, but with the essential component being a strong sense of ethics and public service. An ethical basis to the operation of finance is not a constraint or limitation on the finance sector, but rather the condition that governs the existence of the financial system. Professionals within the sector should remain cognisant of this dynamic, and companies should work to develop an accepted understanding of, and respect for, the role of regulation and legislation in contributing to the fulfilment of the finance sector's public service obligations.

4

THE TWIST

Duties

Clare Payne

DUTIES AND OBLIGATIONS

Individuals, as employees, are subject to certain duties such as performing specific tasks, fulfilling reporting requirements, working standard hours, and obeying particular laws and regulations that apply to their area of work. In addition, organisations may require a commitment to company values, practices and codes. Confidentiality is another duty owed to the employer as well as customers and clients, and is critical in ensuring a trusted finance sector. On their part, organisations are also subject to duties, such as the provision of a safe working environment, adequate support and guidance for staff, and adherence to statutory entitlements such as annual and sick leave.

In finance, there are common duties and obligations for individuals that serve to protect both the employer and, importantly, the integrity of the financial system. These include provisions relating to:

- dealing on personal account—for example, trading while working for a bank is strictly regulated

- avoiding conflicts of interest—individuals must advise of affiliations, previous dealings and external directorships that might result in a conflict
- intellectual property restrictions—these cover trade secrets, client lists and confidential information
- notice and non-competes—extended notice periods and 'gardening leave' are common practice to ensure markets are not compromised by the use of insider information.

The Chartered Financial Analyst Institute (CFA), a global association of investment professionals, outlines five areas relating to duties to clients:

1. loyalty, prudence and care
2. fair dealing
3. suitability
4. performance presentation
5. preservation of confidentiality.[1]

Loyalty refers to the avoidance of conflicts and compensation incentives that can result in action being taken that is not in the client's interests. Loyalty also includes the preserving of confidentiality of information and the refusal of gifts or offers that can affect independence and objectivity. Prudence relates to the exercising of caution and discretion in balancing risk and return. Care simply involves avoiding harm to clients.

Fair dealing covers the duty of members to deal fairly and objectively when providing investment analysis and recommendations, taking investment action, or engaging in other professional activities. Suitability refers to the duty to make a reasonable inquiry prior to making investment recommendations. Members must ensure that investments are suitable to the client, consistent with the client's objectives, and consider the total portfolio.

Performance presentation relates to the communication of investment information. Reasonable efforts must be made to ensure communications are fair, accurate and complete. Preservation of confidentiality covers the duty to keep current, former and prospective client information confidential, with exceptions for illegal activities, when required by law and when permission is granted by the client.

General duties imposed by the *Corporations Act* of Australia on directors and officers of companies include:

- the duty to exercise powers and duties with the care and diligence that a reasonable person would have which includes taking steps to ensure they are properly informed about the financial position of the company and ensuring the company doesn't trade if it is insolvent
- the duty to exercise powers and duties in good faith in the best interests of the company and for a proper purpose
- the duty not to improperly use their position to gain an advantage for themselves or someone else, or to cause detriment to the company
- the duty not to improperly use information obtained through their position to gain an advantage for themselves or someone else, or to cause detriment to the company.[2]

In addition to general duties, there are specific fiduciary duties for directors, trustees and individuals in particular positions of authority.

FIDUCIARY DUTIES

A fiduciary duty is underpinned by a fiduciary relationship, which can be defined as a person having full trust and confidence in another to act in their interests rather than out of self-interest. Many financial services providers are subject to a statutory obligation to act in the 'best interests' of their clients (see the section on 'best interests' later in this chapter'). This requirement applies to:

- a financial adviser providing personal financial product advice to retail clients—section 961B(1) of the *Corporations Act 2001* imposes a duty on a person who provides personal advice to a retail client to act in the best interests of the client in relation to the advice
- the responsible entity of a registered managed investment scheme (MIS)—the obligation is owed to the investors in the MIS through section 601FC(1)(c) of the *Corporations Act*.
- the trustee of a superannuation fund—the obligation is owed to the beneficiaries of the fund according to section 52(2)(c) of the *Superannuation Industry (Supervision) (SIS) Act 1993*. The directors of the corporate trustee owe their duties both to the company and, under section 52A, to the beneficiaries directly.

EFFICIENTLY, HONESTLY AND FAIRLY

There is a general duty for Australian financial services licence holders to act efficiently, honestly and fairly in accordance with section 912A(1)(a) of the *Corporations Act*. The focus of the provision is on the reasonable standard of performance which the public is entitled to expect of a licensee.[3] Importantly, the 'efficiently, honestly and fairly' standard can be breached by conduct which is not criminal but which is morally wrong in a commercial sense.[4]

DUE CARE AND DILIGENCE

Directors and officers have a duty to exercise care and diligence in the discharge of their duties, under section 180(1) of the *Corporations Act*. Specifically, in their pursuit of the company's best interests, directors are held to the standard of due care and diligence that a reasonable director would exercise in the circumstances.

A 'business judgement rule' defence is contained in subsection 180(2), with a business judgement defined as any decision to take or not take action in respect of a matter relevant to the business operations of the company. The essence of the rule is that a director or officer of a company will be taken to have met the requirements of the duty of care and diligence, both under the legislation and at general law, in making a business judgement if the director or officer:
- made the judgement in good faith for a proper purpose
- did not have a material personal interest in the subject matter of the judgement
- informed himself or herself about the subject matter of the judgement to the extent he or she reasonably believed to be appropriate
- rationally believed that the judgement was in the best interests of the company.

That said, no such defence is available for a breach of trustee directors' duties under section 52A of the *SIS Act*.

It is important to note that governance inaction by fiduciaries on issues that present a foreseeable financial risk to their company may not satisfy the duty of due care and diligence (nor the business judgement rule defence). Minter Ellison special counsel Sarah Barker explained in the 2015 article 'Institutional Investment, Corporate Governance and Climate Change: What Is a Trustee to do?' that common reasons for governance inaction on material issues might not satisfy duty of care and diligence, even with subjective good faith. This applies to reasons such as denial or scepticism, (honest) ignorance, unreflective assumption, uncertainty or complexity paralysis, benchmarking to peers or regulatory compliance, and conscious cost–benefit based on outdated assumptions or methodologies that are not fit for their forward-looking purpose.[5]

It is the process of information gathering and deliberation that is critical to satisfying the duty of due care and diligence. The decision that results from that process—for example, to invest or divest—is not the determinative issue. Rather, the relevant inquiry is whether, in their oversight of fund performance against its objectives, a trustee, director or fiduciary is appropriately informed and engaged with relevant risks and opportunities, has sought expert advice where appropriate, has applied independent judgement to the matters at hand, and has constructively evaluated the strategic consequences of material issues using methodologies and assumptions that are appropriate for their forward-looking purpose.

BEST INTERESTS

The term 'best interests' is one of continuing inquiry as trustees, directors and fiduciaries attempt to determine the extent of their responsibilities and whether 'best interests' implies the pursuit of purely financial benefit. However, according to recent legal interpretations, 'best interests' should not be interpreted as 'best outcome'. A beneficiary will potentially have a wide range of interests, perhaps acknowledged in the fact that legislation expressly refers to interests in the plural.

This was affirmed by Michelle Levy, a partner in Allens law firm:

> What really does matter is that the best interests duty is not interpreted as a duty to obtain the best outcome. Despite some very clear statements by many judges including in the High Court that the covenant [in the *SIS Act*] is concerned with ensuring the trustee is free to exercise its powers and discharge its duties for their proper purpose (without any unauthorised conflict or profit)—the idea that the duty in fact requires trustees of superannuation funds to achieve good outcomes for beneficiaries persists.[6]

The Australian Government initiative MySuper is intended to provide low-cost and simple super products that employers can choose as their default super funds. The duty of the trustee here is to design a MySuper product that it considers is reasonably likely to provide returns at a reasonable cost to MySuper members. On this Levy wrote, 'I don't think it requires the trustee to design a product that will obtain the best possible result for members (the highest return at the lowest cost)'.

For advisers, the satisfying of the duty of best interests relates to the process the adviser undertakes in providing the advice, and not to the content of the advice itself.

LEGAL DEVELOPMENTS AND INTERPRETATIONS

As directors, trustees and other fiduciaries seek to understand their obligations, and advocates of responsible investment seek to challenge narrow interpretations of fiduciary duties, there is increasing reference to the 2005 report *A Legal Framework for the Integration of Environmental, Social and Governance Issues into Institutional Investment*, otherwise known as the Freshfields Report. The UN Environment Programme Finance Initiative (UNEP FI) Asset Management Working Group commissioned the report from Freshfields Bruckhaus Deringer, an international law firm. On fiduciary duty, the report said:

> In our opinion, it may be a breach of fiduciary duties to fail to take account of ESG considerations that are relevant and to give them appropriate weight, bearing in mind that some important economic analysts and leading financial institutions are satisfied that a strong link between good ESG performance and good financial performance exists.[7]

The report covered the nine jurisdictions of Australia, Canada, France, Germany, Italy, Japan, Spain, the United Kingdom and the United States, and concluded that 'integrating ESG considerations into an investment analysis so as to more reliably predict financial performance is clearly permissible and is arguably required in all jurisdictions'.[8]

There are also lessons for directors, trustees and other fiduciaries in more recent cases. The *James Hardie* proceedings against the directors and executives in *ASIC v Hellicar*[9] and the *Centro* case of *ASIC v Healey & Ors*[10] are considered to have delivered two vital lessons for fiduciaries:

1. There are limits to the protection from liability that is afforded by delegation, and by reliance on the advice of committees and experts.
2. Directors cannot delegate away responsibility for their core, irreducible responsibilities.[11]

In 2014, the UK Law Commission report *Fiduciary Duties of Investment Intermediaries* also provided clarity on fiduciary duties in concluding that 'the law is sufficiently flexible to allow other, subordinate concerns to be taken into account ... provided that: they have good reason to think that scheme members share the concern; and there is no risk of significant financial detriment to the fund'.[12]

According to the 2015 report *Fiduciary Duty in the 21st Century*, which was published by the organisation Principles for Responsible Investment (PRI), 'Fiduciary duty is not an obstacle to action on environmental, social and governance factors'. The report looked at fiduciary duty across eight markets—Australia, Brazil, Canada, Germany, Japan, South Africa, the United Kingdom and the United States—using a series of events, interviews, case studies and a legal review. Fiona Reynolds, the managing director of PRI, was quoted as saying:

> Recent studies have broadened the interpretation of fiduciary duty away from the narrow confines of past definitions, and have emphasised that there is no conflict between fiduciary duty and ESG considerations—there is a growing recognition that ESG issues are in fact financially material to a portfolio. Using the status quo as a reason for not integrating ESG is no longer acceptable.[13]

An area that lawyers are monitoring is the overstatement of the 'responsible' characteristics of an investment product or policy, or ineffectual policy implementation, as this may expose the trustee, directors and other fiduciaries to claims that they have misled their fund beneficiaries or the market. This could be the next area to challenge the concept of fiduciary duty and act as a warning for trustees, directors and other fiduciaries who have considered their duty as being the delivery of financial benefits, at any cost.

DUTIES AS AN EMPLOYER

Employers are also subject to duties to their staff. These cover health and safety, and include the obligation to ensure the work environment is free from discrimination and harassment. There is now an increased focus on diversity through a range of initiatives designed to ensure that workforces are representative of the larger population, and that barriers to the advancement of different groups of people are addressed.

Employers have a duty to provide a safe working environment for their employees, contractors and visitors. Legislation and programs have traditionally focused on health and safety (previously known as occupational health and safety). Legislation in Australia provides for minimum standards that aim to prevent injury and disease in workplaces. Common features of state-based legislation include:

- provision of systems of work that are safe and without risk to health
- prevention of injury and disease through the elimination or minimisation of risks
- work representation, consultation, cooperation and issue resolution.

There has been an evident shift in sections of the corporate environment to a broader concept of workplace health and safety. Workplace 'wellbeing' programs, which are common to organisations in the finance sector, focus on a work–life balance, support for parental and carer's responsibilities, and mental health, in addition to minimum standards.

According to the Australian Psychological Society (APS), individuals spend a third of their lives at work. Therefore, it is crucial to people's health and wellbeing that work is a positive experience. The APS Stress and Wellbeing surveys conducted from 2011 to 2016 found that problems at work can have an enormous impact on an individual's mental health and wellbeing, and that levels of workplace stress remain high.[14] In addition, organisational psychology research shows that creating a positive working environment also has business benefits— again we see the making of a 'business case', an economic justification for what otherwise might be termed common sense.

Business in the Community, a UK-based organisation that's part of the Prince's Responsible Business Network, recently undertook a national survey and used the results to produce the *Mental Health at Work*

Report 2016. The report called for employers to recognise the scale of poor mental health in the workplace and take significant steps to reduce the risk of their business being a contributor. It highlighted the duty of care of employers to their employees to respond to mental ill health just as they would to a physical illness. It also called for organisations to equip managers with the tools, support and organisational culture they need to do their job well, including managing employees with mental health issues.[15]

Case Study
National Australia Bank

Financial institutions in Australia such National Australia Bank (NAB) have said that they are committed to safeguarding the health and wellbeing of their employees, customers and the broader community. NAB has acknowledged that health, particularly mental health, is the subject of increasing concern in the community and a key issue for the financial services sector.

Through a series of targeted initiatives, the bank aims to better equip its employees and customers in responding to the circumstances they face. As such, it offers a range of tools, resources, services and programs to assist people in managing their physical health and mental wellbeing. The approach includes a strong focus on early intervention to deal with physical or psychological illness and injury, a range of mental health initiatives supported by an Employee Assistance Program, flexible work practices, an influenza vaccination program, and other programs.[16]

At a broader level, NAB has collaborated with insurance industry peers to develop mental health training for customers who hold life insurance. This follows moves by the Australian insurance industry regulator to raise mental health awareness.

In order to support customers better, NAB has developed a centralised reporting system to capture incidents involving customers threatening self-harm. This data will assist the industry to create effective and targeted support strategies.

NAB also actively promotes a program called Heads Up that supports small- and medium-sized business customers. Heads Up provides free tools and resources developed by the Mentally Healthy Workplace Alliance and beyondblue. Customers are also offered access to an NAB counselling partner in times of crisis; for example, in the event of a natural disaster.

Such programs are reflective of a broader understanding and acceptance of the obligations of financial institutions to their staff and society.

DIVERSITY IN THE WORKPLACE AND WORKFORCE

McKinsey & Company, in its 2015 report *Diversity Matters*, identified that diverse companies—those in the top quartile for gender, race and ethnic diversity—are better able to improve their customer orientation. The report also confirmed that diversity can assist in decision-making.[17] These conclusions provide yet more compelling reasons for financial institutions to prioritise diversity, particularly as they navigate the professionalisation of the sector.

According to the Australian Government's Workplace Gender Equality Agency, strategies that promote workplace gender equality specifically minimise a company's risk of financial and reputational loss as a result of lawsuits caused by discriminatory conduct.[18] Inclusive and respectful workplaces, where gender diversity is valued, directly reduce the risks of employee litigation and can avoid the negative impact sexual harassment has on absenteeism, team conflict, and morale at work.[19]

There has been a range of studies on diversity over recent decades and the business case—the economic and financial justification for diversity within workplaces—is now well established and commonly accepted across the finance sector. However, the implementation of agreed strategies and the achievement of diversity goals has proven more difficult for the sector to achieve.

As a result of increased studies, discussion and generational changes, the understanding of what diversity means has become more detailed, with two groups identified. There are those with 'inherent diversity', such as gender and race, and those with 'acquired diversity', such as global experience and language skills. More recently, organisations have adopted the term 'inclusion', with diversity being one aspect of a broader strategy that relates to both staff and the market.

The Center for Talent Innovation, in its 2013 report *Innovation, Diversity and Market Growth*, found that work cultures that embraced diversity across the two groups led to a 'speak-up' culture where individuals felt comfortable to discuss issues and raise problems, and thus decision-making was improved across the organisation. In addition, the likelihood of expanding market share and the capture of new markets was greater in companies with this two-dimensional diversity.[20]

An inherently diverse workforce can be a potent source of innovation. Diverse individuals have been found to be better attuned to the unmet needs of consumers or clients like themselves. In fact, the insight of these individuals has been thought to be critical in identifying and addressing new market opportunities. The 2013 Center for Talent Innovation report found that when teams comprise one or more members who represent the gender, ethnicity, culture, generation or sexual orientation of the team's target end user, the entire team is far more likely—as much as 158 per cent more likely—to understand that target, increasing their likelihood of innovating effectively for that end user. Such findings were further confirmed in a 2013 study by Deloitte that found business performance was improved in organisations in which levels of diversity and inclusion were high.[21] Diversity therefore plays an important role in ensuring true service to the public.

GENDER DIVERSITY IN FINANCE

Despite numerous studies, much documented evidence and a clear business case for diversity in business, gender diversity remains a particular challenge and an ongoing priority for the finance sector.

The Gender Diversity in Investment Management Survey, conducted by the CFA Institute Research Foundation in 2016, found that compared with their male counterparts, the top female investment professionals globally held only 9.8 per cent of chief executive officer roles, 10.2 per cent of chief investment officer roles, 11 per cent of chief financial officer roles, 14.9 per cent of portfolio manager roles, 15.1 per cent of investment consultant positions, and 17.3 per cent of personal financial adviser or planner roles. Women (22 per cent) were also more likely than men (16 per cent) to have jobs that supported or serviced those in investment management.[22]

While many organisations across the finance sector have initiated programs focused on gender diversity in the hope of altering such statistics, increasingly, industry and professional associations have had to consider the role they can play in assisting the industry to achieve gender diversity. In 2016, for example, Women in Banking and Finance and the Australian Financial Markets Association launched a plan addressing gender diversity at the sector's entry level. They designed a set of initiatives to assist organisations to attract more female graduates into institutional and investment banking roles. A range of industry bodies also worked together to identify other initiatives that would complement existing gender diversity policies in place across the sector.[23]

The Commonwealth Bank of Australia (CBA) is an example of a financial institution that has a public commitment to gender diversity. Through its Diversity in Leadership program, the bank has committed itself to attracting, developing and retaining diverse leaders. Indeed, in 2016, women comprised 60 per cent of the CBA workforce and filled over 45 per cent of its management roles. The strategy used to increase the representation of women in senior leadership roles includes:

- increasing awareness and education
- creating greater transparency in appointments
- updating business processes and policies
- actively working to ensure female leaders are identified early in their career
- attracting and retaining top female talent through initiatives such as mentoring, high-potential development programs, and flexible work, parents' and carers' support options.[24]

A range of other organisations, such as Chief Executive Women, and Women in Banking and Finance, are actively working to both research and promote gender diversity, and have been influential in the increasing prioritisation of diversity on the corporate agenda.

Yet despite such efforts, professional services company Ernst & Young, in a 2016 report titled *Navigating Disruption without Gender Diversity? Think Again*, concluded that financial services organisations weren't doing enough to bring about meaningful change at the most influential levels in relation to diversity. They found that both male and female leaders recognised the industry was in a transition phase, and that 77 per cent of men and 66 per cent of women acknowledged the value of diversity in navigating this industry change. However, four disconnects were identified as holding back gender parity:

1. the reality disconnect—business leaders assume the problem is nearly solved, despite little progress within their own companies

2. the data disconnect—companies do not effectively measure their progress on gender parity
3. the pipeline disconnect—organisations are not creating pipelines for future female leaders
4. the perception and perspective disconnect—men and women do not view the problem in the same way.[25]

In late 2016, CFA Societies Australia, member societies of the CFA Institute, and a global association of investment professionals, called on financial services to lead Australian business as advocates and practitioners of diversity and inclusion, with an initial focus on gender equality. Anthony Serhan, president of the CFA Society Sydney, said that effective diversity practice was one of the hallmarks of a mature industry:

> The world is a diverse place and the principles by which a society's belief system and practices are based must reflect this fact. This isn't just from a moral perspective; there are genuine reasons why diverse societies function not only more harmoniously but also deliver improved concrete outcomes at all levels and constituencies. The principles and outcomes as applied to industry are no different and, as the stewards of community wealth, we want our industry to show leadership in this area.[26]

DIVERSITY AND LANGUAGE

Language plays an important role in shaping business strategies, workplace cultures and the setting of an ethical tone. It is interesting, then, to consider that it is not uncommon for words and terms from other fields, such as the military or construction, to be used in the context of business and finance. For example, a manager might 'rally the troops', have a 'take no prisoners' style, 'launch' a 'counterattack' after establishing a 'bulkhead', or agree not to 'pincer' the competition, who've been 'in the trenches'. They might respect the 'chain of command', recognising those who have 'risen through the ranks'. A manager might draw a 'line in the sand' in an effort to put a 'stake in the ground', signalling a new 'regime' and, importantly, bringing the team closer to 'executing' the 'mission'.

Some have claimed that the use of military metaphors in business serves to exclude women. Raina Brands, assistant professor of organisational behaviour at the London Business School (LBS), in an article for the LBS website in 2014, explained that 'the use of military parlance in organisations may reinforce historically-rooted and implicitly held beliefs that business is no place for a woman'.[27] In other words, the use of such words and terms can inadvertently impact the diversity efforts of organisations by serving to isolate certain groups, or contribute to setting a tone that is counter to that which is desired. For it is not just women who might be affected by the use of terms borrowed from other fields. Those from non-English-speaking backgrounds and multilingual individuals may be less likely to understand such words when they are used in a business context.

In addition to the potential exclusion of specific sectors of the workforce, there should also be concern about the values that may be implied by the use of military terms in the context of finance.

Ensuring that language, particularly the use of 'borrowed terms', does not discriminate against and isolate employees and customers should be a key consideration in business. This applies not just to the communications or marketing department, but to all individuals regardless of their position.

DIVERSITY, THE PAY GAP AND INCENTIVES

It has been well documented that the corporate sector tends to favour a dominant masculine group, and this is particularly evident in financial services. There are many cases of women, as well as racial minorities, experiencing limited opportunities. There is also much evidence of discrimination based on sexual preference.

Wage disparity based on factors other than skills and experience have continued despite long-established anti-discrimination legislation. The Workplace Gender Equality Agency detailed in its *Gender Equity Insights 2016* that the full-time gender pay gap in Australia was around 18 per cent,[28] with women earning on average only 82 per cent of a man's pay.[29] This means that a woman would have to work an additional sixty-five days each year to earn the same as a man.[30]

In an attempt to address this situation, the finance sector is attempting to understand unconscious bias. Nancy DiTomaso, of Rutgers Business School in New Jersey, concluded that 'favouritism or advantage is passed along from those who are already in positions of power, authority, and privilege to those with whom they identify, often know, and usually welcome'.[31] Perhaps it's not surprising that people tend to prefer the company of people like themselves. To counter this inclination, organisations are implementing explicit measures, and in some cases incentives, to encourage diversity, particularly regarding the managers of teams. Measures of performance include the reflection of diversity in recruitment and promotion.

Diversity in this context is not limited to gender but also focuses on race and socioeconomic background, and there are increasing discussions as to the benefits of diversity of life experience. Nigel Bassett-Jones, of Oxford Brookes University School, posited that a diverse team is one that is open to different points of view. He concluded that such teams are better able to critically evaluate situations and exercise superior decision-making and problem solving.[32]

In 2016, a report was released by the Australian Human Rights Commission (AHRC) in partnership with Sydney University Business School, Westpac, PwC Australia and Telstra titled *Leading for Change: A Blueprint for Cultural Diversity and Inclusive Leadership*. Dr Tim Soutphommasane, AHRC race discrimination commissioner, outlined during the launch of the report that while nearly 50 per cent of the Australian population was either born overseas,[33] or had a parent who was born overseas, and an estimated 10 per cent of the Australian population had Asian cultural origins or ancestry,[34] such diversity was far from proportionately represented when it came to positions of leadership in both the public and private sectors. Dr Soutphommasane called for a more inclusive style, as 'there could be bias—especially unconsciously—where leaders tend to seek what they know'.

In recognition of the diversity of staff backgrounds and needs, organisations are now considering how to appropriately incentivise and reward their employees. Some companies have elected to provide employees with flexible benefit plans that allow individuals to select particular options such as free child care or additional leave in exchange for a reduced salary. Such programs allow employees to tailor their remuneration and benefits package to the demands of their particular life.[35] These plans will likely assist employees to feel they are being treated equally, without employers necessarily needing to treat them identically.

THE ETHICS OF REDUNDANCIES AND TERMINATION OF EMPLOYMENT

Scenes of sacked finance executives walking out of an office carrying a box with their personal belongings are commonplace, as are stories of individuals leaving immediately when advised that their employment has been terminated. Some claim this is the price one pays for working in finance, a just deserts of sorts, but is it ethical?

Management and human resources staff tend to justify these swift 'exits' by referencing risk, particularly around confidentiality of information. It is claimed the risk of an employee going back to their desk and copying files, sending malicious emails, disrupting a deal, making illegal trades or, for those in money-managing roles, actually stealing, is so great that they must be marched out of the building. The belief is that all this is possible regarding an employee who, the day before, had access to files or trading systems and was handing out a business card as a representative of the company.

A small percentage of people working in finance are traders. When justifying the finance style of termination, people—even within the sector—seem to mention traders, in that it is certainly justified for a trader to be marched out without any warning. However, simple steps can be taken to limit access to trading and computer systems. In a matter of minutes, a trader's access can be restricted or cut so they can no longer impact the market. Access to emails can be instantly revoked for all staff. Perhaps it's time for the sector to apply its IT acumen to restoring some dignity to the termination process.

Terminations should be a last resort for an employer, reluctantly considered and actioned after all other options, such as part-time work, job sharing and leave without pay, have been considered. It is curious that while some of the most highly qualified mathematicians, actuaries and strategists work in finance, there is little evidence that teams are consulted or given the opportunity to workshop among themselves how the desired reductions could be achieved while maintaining the cohesion and effective functioning of the business.

Modern workplaces tend to operate under a somewhat transparent and accepted class system, with different benefits attaching to positions in the organisational hierarchy. There are the obvious distinctions of titles and responsibilities in the business sense. However, there are also other benefits, not necessarily written or acknowledged. Directors, for example, will almost certainly have access to a parking spot in the building. The CEO will likely have a reserved spot on the first floor of the car park, spared the hassle of winding down to the lower levels where the rest of senior management are relegated. The chair may even have someone park their car for them.

Department heads and team leaders may have someone fetch their coffee in the morning—executive assistants are likely to take orders for the whole team, their status in the organisation clear to everyone, including the barista. Those wishing to work their way up will only buy coffee for themselves, never offering to buy for others for fear of being further down the pecking order.

This class (and hence benefit) system extends to most facets of a person's working life in finance, in particular termination. The more senior is an individual, the more dignity is applied to the process. For senior executives, a termination is likely to be cloaked in mild language and is rarely framed as a redundancy. 'Taking time off', 'Pursuing other interests', 'Allowing others to lead', 'Prioritising family' or quite simply 'Retirement' are common explanations, variously applied even to obviously underperforming senior executives.

Senior executives are also afforded the opportunity to wind down, to say goodbye, to mentally process their impending departure. From a business perspective they do a handover, tie up loose ends and ensure the smooth transition of matters. They have farewells; the CEO tends to send out an email to staff 'explaining' the departure, and the individuals tend to do a mailout to their friends, colleagues and business acquaintances, letting them know that they are moving on and offering their future contact details. On many occasions, they will also receive a gift from the organisation and will most certainly get an extensively negotiated financial package that eases any related stress around the change.

That's what it's like for senior executives. For those below this mystery mark, they may be marched off the premises and no longer welcome at the team lunch for which they accepted an invitation just a week ago.

Organisations want to employ the best people they can find. Recruitment processes are thorough, involving background checks, behavioural interviews and in some cases psychometric testing. Throughout their time with an organisation, staff are then inducted and consistently developed through both internal and external training programs. Ultimately, these staff are entrusted with representing the company, and the development process reassures management their staff can be trusted.

One is left to wonder why the finance sector is so distrusting of its own staff once they have been advised of their termination. It is clear that despite the best recruitment practices and development programs, in many cases management do not in fact trust their staff, those below senior management that is.

Career-minded individuals seek to develop a professional reputation. In some instances, an individual's reputation is so strong that clients move with them as they change jobs. They can become experts in their own right, transcending the organisation for which they work. It leads one to speculate whether such individuals would risk committing fraud or sending out a malicious email on advice of their termination. Even aspiring executives have their futures to consider, a future they wish to have in the sector, and such an event would not be a desired part of a good career story.

Of course, there is also pride to consider. Regardless of how this corporate pride may be demonstrated—by the designer cufflinks, the perfectly pressed shirt or the overzealous issuing of business cards—it is a factor that can certainly serve to curb inappropriate or damaging behaviour. But it would appear that management find it difficult to rely on pride and trust in giving them comfort around the risks that stem from redundancies and terminations. This is the case even though there are various, well-established legal protections for employers when it comes to terminating employees and protecting intellectual property. An employee cannot simply take a client list, nor can one legally copy documents or systems. Most employees are made aware of this fact in their employment contracts at the commencement of the job, and if they were to be reminded again at termination, then temptation would further abate.

When assessing decisions and actions from an ethical perspective, the justification that 'This is the way we do things around here' or 'It's what everyone else does' can be troubling. Processes and rituals are important to organisational cultures; however, when such rituals spread across a sector, there is a risk of unintended adaptions and inappropriate applications. One would be wise to ask, 'Why do we do it like this, and is it right?'

Terminations and redundancies are likely to continue across the finance sector as it adapts and evolves with society. It should therefore remain a priority for the sector to reconsider the process they use for terminations and contemplate how to adjust their workforce while maintaining the dignity of once-essential individuals. This is particularly important as the sector considers how it can support the mental health and wellbeing of its people.

The 'walkout' practice in terminating an individual's employment is certainly efficient. Hundreds of staff can be dealt with in a matter of hours. The process is cold and can be clinical, but some may ask if it is unrealistic to expect anything different from a corporation, particularly one that deals with largely quantifiable matters. It is, however, the human collective within an organisation that forms its conscience. Organisations are also shaped by the consciences of the shareholders, board members, clients and consumers—all of them have feelings. This fact should not be forgotten in the push for efficient downsizing and adjustments prompted by changing market conditions.

People also have memories. If, or perhaps when, the market turns and companies are again looking to hire, will the same people who were marched off the premises be willing to take up employment again? Or will it be at this time that corporations discover those former employees on the other side of deals, such as that young graduate who no-one spoke to progressing to a senior executive of a client, with the certainty that they will never cooperate with their former employer and, in fact, will ensure they steer their business elsewhere. This is something leaders would be wise to think about when agreeing on how they should treat their once-valued staff, especially in finance where every employee is potentially a client, whether it be by virtue of a bank account, home loan or credit card.

Perhaps this risk will be motivation enough to change the behaviour of senior management and human resources professionals within banking and finance, as well as that of the employment lawyers and outplacement providers who advise them.

DUTIES TO STAKEHOLDERS

Dr Simon Longstaff of The Ethics Centre routinely highlights the importance of the distinction between wants, interests and needs, particularly in the context of service to clients and the prioritising of stakeholders. A need is something we must have in order to live a recognisably human life. An interest, however, relates to whether something is useful for one's benefit or advantage. By way of example, if health is something that one needs, then taking medicine might be in one's interests. A want, on the other hand, involves something that one desires, whether or not one actually needs it or has an interest to serve.

Steve Tucker, a founding director of The Banking and Finance Oath, explained his involvement in the oath in an interview where he said that, over his twenty-five years in financial services, 'I have always been very concerned about ensuring that above all else, our clients could trust that we are working in their best interests'. Unfortunately, there have been many cases of decisions and actions in business, including the finance sector, where misconduct has been justified on the basis of serving the 'interests' of a particular stakeholder. In fact, Christine Lagarde from the IMF, in an address at the Federal Bank of New York in November 2015, said, 'If the financial industry is to put people before profits, and society before shareholders, we need to see a change in values and behavior in individuals themselves'.

Mark Rantall, CEO of the Financial Planning Association (FPA), in an article he wrote in 2014 on the importance of trust, said:

> It is critical when your profession is based on a foundation of trust that you do everything to enshrine that trust, protect it and promote it. This idea of protecting trust helped lead the FPA to advance its vision to 'stand with Australians for a better financial future'. The critical word here is 'with'. It means advisers need to be the advocates for their clients, by sitting on their side of the desk with them and not with any other party. That means that you put the clients' interest ahead of all others. That is the heart of acting in the clients' best interest.[36]

As the retail banking sector comes under increasing scrutiny for its lending practices, particularly in relation to mortgages (covering the appropriateness of both the amount lent as well as the method of repayment), the question of whose interests have been served (often seen to be those of the financial institution rather than the customer) will be central to inquiries and likely to shape future regulations.

It is clear that in the finance sector, behaving ethically has a great deal to do with appropriately weighing up the interests of stakeholders. Problems are likely to occur in balancing company, shareholder and customer interests. This is where good decision-making and ethical practices, as outlined in Chapter 7, play an important role. (Also see Chapter 2 for commentary on the evolution of the consideration of stakeholders in business.)

THE LANGUAGE OF STAKEHOLDER ENGAGEMENT

As stakeholder engagement becomes an expected, routine business practice across the finance sector, it is important for individuals with such a responsibility to consider how to effectively communicate with different individuals and groups. Customers, for example, as one of these stakeholder groups, will invariably come from different parts of the community, and have differing levels of competency in English and varying levels of financial literacy. So the approach and language regarded as appropriate to communicate with these different groups will vary. In particular, those managing the process should be aware of the impact of language selection on the ability to effectively engage and thus determine and understand the wants, interests and needs of the stakeholders.

According to an article by Raymond MacKenzie, professor of English at the University of Saint Thomas in Minnesota, the language chosen to communicate with stakeholders either helps to forge bonds of community or it erodes community, infecting it with a generalised distrust that can even metastasise into open conflict.[37]

Dr Mark Shaw, a radiation oncologist with the Peter MacCallum Cancer Centre in Melbourne, attended a community engagement forum held so he and other residents could respond to a building proposal for the area. As the developer talked of 'meeting minimum regulations' and 'not breaching any standards', Dr Shaw felt compelled to stand up when given the opportunity to speak. He said, 'I'm a cancer doctor, and if you became a patient of mine tomorrow and came to my room at the hospital for an appointment and I said to you, "I will provide you with the minimum care I am required to", would you think that was enough?' The developer's choice of language to explain their decision-making might have been appropriate for a report to an internal audit department or peers in the industry. However, communicated to a group of concerned members of the community, it only served to isolate rather than engage this important group of stakeholders.

Businesses, particularly those in the finance sector, have become increasingly aware of the ease with which customers can voice their concerns and dissatisfaction through the use of social media. Consumers, activists and even employees can take immediate, direct action when they believe decisions are unfair or unethical. This development places even more importance on having a considered process for stakeholder engagement.

Effective stakeholder engagement can lead to higher-quality decision-making; improve risk-management practices by allowing risks to be identified and considered earlier, thereby reducing future costs; and, importantly, ensure that products and services actually meet customer needs. Therefore, the attention being given to each aspect of the process, including the language used, should be monitored to ensure that trust is built rather than jeopardised.

CONCLUSION

Although many of the duties of employers and employees are legislated and formalised in regulations, they are still subject to interpretation and can be seen to evolve with developments in business and society more broadly. Both employers and employees need to remain conscious of changes not just in the rules but also the expectations of a range of stakeholders. Understanding and respecting duties is critical to attracting and retaining staff as well as investment, and of course, it is essential in maintaining trust.

5

INTO TEMPTATION

Conflicts of Interest

Paul Kofman

A cynic might say that you can hardly expect somebody to act in your best interests when you entrust them with your money. If that's true, then why are we still surprised by finance professionals who do not seem to prioritise their customers' interests? In the days when you had a close personal connection with your local bank, its manager would be the custodian of your best interests. And you could hold them to account, as the bank and its manager were an integral part of the community. But with bank branches closing and transactions going online, that close personal relationship has fractured and virtually disappeared.

So how can you be sure that your bank still looks after your interests and satisfies your rights as a customer? Legal enforcement certainly helps, but it is often expensive, time-consuming and, as the law is an impartial arbiter, does not necessarily prioritise customers' interests. A regulator could intervene, but its prime purpose of protecting the integrity of the financial system and its markets—acting in the public interest— may compromise customers' best interests. Regulatory intervention is also expensive and often lacks legal clout. A government-appointed ombudsman with the sole objective of protecting customers' rights seems fit for purpose. But again, establishing the office is expensive and it often lacks the necessary legal bite.

An alignment of interests would clearly be the cheapest and most efficient way to achieve customer trust. That alignment may be hard to establish in a one-off transaction, but it is the promise of repeat transactions that elevates customer interest in banks. A happy, satisfied customer is more likely to return for business. But if that customer is already 'locked up' (for example, in a long-term contract with restrictive breakage clauses), or there is little chance of repeat business, should the bank not extract the maximum value from the transaction and pursue self-interest?

According to economist and philosopher Adam Smith, the alignment of interests comes about automatically as long as individuals rationally pursue self-interest.[1] To achieve common interests through self-interest, you need free, competitive, efficient and transparent markets and institutions. Even in Smith's days—in the eighteenth century—these preconditions were often violated, or at least were less than perfect. Interests do in fact compete, requiring intervention to achieve alignment. Financial institutions know this. Consider, for example, Investcorp, a global alternative investment fund manager which structures its corporate governance based on three principles: alignment of interests, transparency of reporting, and collective decision-making. The company's website reads: 'A central tenet of Investcorp's philosophy is to ensure that interests among shareholders, clients and management are optimally aligned and that lender interests are well protected'.[2]

A conflict of interest arises where two or more competing interests collide, whereby one's actions to pursue their own interests harms or disadvantages the other's interests. Conflicts of interest have always existed in business, with private, customer, institutional and public interests competing for favour. Consider the financial adviser who recommends the bank's 'reverse mortgage almond trees investment scheme' to her pensioner clients. Whose interests is the financial adviser pursuing? The employer's? Personal interest? And whose interests are downgraded or altogether ignored? The clients'? The finance sector's? The public's? There could certainly be tension here.

Wayne Overall, executive director of managed investment scheme Almond Investors Limited, was quoted in *The Australian* in 2011 as saying:

> The real cost of food is going up significantly in coming decades as populations and incomes rise in the developing world. With the health benefits of almonds increasingly well known, the fundamentals for almonds are strong and can only get better. Investors who want a genuine income that is not correlated with the stock market or property can see the attraction of a soft commodity like almonds.

Many financial planners have 'run a mile from these schemes' because of high-profile collapses, said Overall, but he added that a lot of advisers and accountants 'understand them well' and like what they can add to an investment portfolio.[3]

Most of the time, those competing interests are held in check by the fear of losing reputation (personal and/or institutional) or by legal and regulatory requirements—and, of course, often by ethical behaviour. But while potential conflicts can be managed, it is difficult to avoid them altogether in the course of doing business. Even with alignment, it is still possible that prioritising one set of interests over another (relatively) disadvantages the other.

Whenever one makes a decision that affects one's own interests, employer's interests or a customer's interests, one needs to consider the possibility of competing interests. When a business requires its employees to act in one party's best interests, say as a trustee for a superannuation fund, then employees will have to suspend all other interests, including their own. Those rules seem to be clear-cut: first comes the duty to the customer, and only then comes the duty to the employer, before personal interests are even considered. But where does that leave public interest? And what to do when one is the investment banker for two corporate customers and one makes a takeover bid for the other?

Interestingly, the existence and appearance of conflicts of interest is much more transparent nowadays than it was in the past. Regulatory and legal intervention has led most financial institutions to formally lodge and declare any potential conflicts as standard operating procedure. Companies and their employees have an obligation to avoid conflicts of interest, as stipulated by the companies' codes of conduct or perhaps a standalone conflict-of-interest policy.

Yet, at the same time as these conflicts are being identified and declared, some may claim they are increasingly going unchecked. Too many examples of inappropriate prioritisation of interest have left the impression that as long as a conflict is formally disclosed, there is no real need to do anything further about it. That could either be interpreted as 'We will do the right thing' or 'You make up your own mind—you have been warned'. The buyer-beware obligation is imposed on the customer who, of course, can only hope for the best, or discount any possible disadvantage or harm that could arise from a conflict of interest.

KNOWING YOUR CONFLICTS OF INTEREST

Common sense suggests that conflicts of interest should be avoided as they can quickly compromise ethics. Even with the best of intentions— through full disclosure and careful management—there are bound to be lingering suspicions of unethical behaviour which undermine trust. Only a strict utilitarian who suspends notions of fairness and justice could possibly argue that as long as on aggregate the outcome is positive, a conflict can be ethically justified.

To better understand and manage the ethical implications of conflicts of interest, we first need to identify them. And they might not be as obvious as we think. Businesspeople (and lawyers) caught in an alleged conflict of interest often claim they were unaware of its existence.

In a 2014 blog post, the Melbourne-based Legal Practitioners' Liability Committee mentioned that a review of its claims experience showed that

> practitioners who act for multiple parties in a matter are often caught unawares by conflicts, which can be difficult to anticipate and arise before the practitioner has realised the danger. Consequently, the practitioner is left exposed to allegations of breach of the rules and duties at common law and in equity, as well as allegations they preferred the interests of one client over another.[4]

First, we must distinguish between potential, actual and perceived conflicts of interest. Potential conflicts might occur, actual conflicts are occurring, and perceived conflicts are judged on their appearance to the outside world but need not be actual.

As investment banks routinely represent multiple corporations competing within a single industry, situations will occur where a conflict between two customers' (multiple parties') interests is simply unavoidable. A takeover will pit bidder against target, yet the investment bank is supposed to endeavour to do its best for both clients. It would, of course, not be possible to run a business by avoiding all potential conflicts of interest. But at least in a very competitive finance sector, the bidder (or the target) has the opportunity to seek independent advice. With the increasing conglomeration of the finance industry, a lack of competition concentrates potentially competing interests—and conflicts quickly become actual. Perceived (apparent) conflicts are by and large a consequence of a lack of trust in the finance sector. The public is already sceptical of the sincerity of a denial of conflict.

Second, individual conflicts are distinct from organisational conflicts. A functional role in an organisation may create a conflict with other functions in that organisation. Again, the conglomeration of the finance industry has created institutions that work in the interests of customers (for example, by providing them with analyst advice on share purchases) at the same time as they work in the interest of corporations (by selling their shares to the customers). Similarly, tying the compensation of a financial advisory division to assets-under-management with their funds management division, creates the conditions that make it all the more likely that the customer's interests will not be prioritised.

When conflicts of interest start influencing decision-making—for example, through shortlisting preferred clients, passing on confidential information, granting special conditions, awarding business, enabling pricing discounts and so on—they manifest themselves in the following behaviours.

The most common outcome of a conflict of interest is *biased judgement*, a direct threat to objectivity in decision-making. An equity analyst accepting hospitality from a corporate client might be more likely to give a positive value appraisal of that corporate's investment proposal. A mortgage specialist might be tempted to extend a home loan to a close relative, despite undocumented or unverified income statements.

A *neglect of the fiduciary duty to clients* is less common but is more severely unethical and mostly illegal. As defined by the law firm Stimmel, Stimmel & Smith, fiduciary duty is the highest set of obligations that one can owe to another.[5] (See the discussion of fiduciary duty in Chapter 4.) The fiduciary (the financial institution) must act in the best interests of the beneficiary (the client) at all times. It cannot take any action that intentionally harms the beneficiary and it must also avoid negligently harming the interests of the beneficiary. This implies that the fiduciary's interests (personal or institutional) cannot supersede the beneficiary's interests. Not only does this require full disclosure of potential conflicts of interest, it also requires the immediate removal of actual conflicts of interest.

Increasingly more common is the issue of access to comprehensive client data, which may cause a *violation of confidentiality*. Having access to a client's banking transactions, a financial adviser may target specific clients with specific investment or loan products, even though banks' codes of conduct (and consumer protection) preclude the use of information acquired in confidence. This has become a much more serious problem of late with the availability of advanced data analytics, whereby financial institutions have the ability to effectively link up and analyse client information (savings accounts, credit cards, home loans, insurance policies and so on).

A fairly common cause of conflicts of interest is *abuse of position*. The ability to grant favours and/or to override procedures (written into the code of conduct) makes potential conflicts very likely. Examples include the lead underwriter in a securities issue who has the power and opportunity to allocate shares in an initial public offering (IPO) to preferred clients, and senior individuals in a bank who overrule a junior colleague's decision to deny a business loan to a close business partner, despite a poor credit rating. Note that abuse of position is not necessarily related to seniority. The functional role itself may create the conditions and opportunity for a conflict of interest. Consider, for example, a statistician employed at the Australian Bureau of Statistics who computes the latest economic indicators and releases the information privately to a friend who then commits insider trading using that information (insider trading is discussed in more detail later in this chapter).[6]

An employee who puts their private interests ahead of their employer's puts themselves in *direct competition* with the employer. Standard employment contracts routinely prohibit this, even when disclosed. Employees of financial institutions are allowed to hold share portfolios and to trade on their own account (although trading opportunities are strictly controlled and monitored). However, someone's role as a corporate adviser in merger negotiations may provide one with material inside information. Using that information to trade for personal benefit would be a violation of duty to the employer and the integrity of the markets (for more on duties and obligations, see Chapter 4).

These behaviours are often legally suspect and at least unethical, meaning they contravene a code of ethics. They leave the impression that finance professionals do not prioritise clients' interests where that is mandated, nor an employer's interests where that is contractually due, and do not look after the broader public interest. They taint the financial system, making it appear unfair, unjust and untrustworthy.

CLASSIC CONFLICTS IN FINANCE

At times it may appear that conflicts of interest are rife in the finance sector.[7] Do they occur more frequently in finance than in other professions? Not necessarily. Consider the dentist recommending his patients use the expensive desensitising toothpaste brand favoured by a friendly supplier, or the intertwined interests emblemised by the revolving door between government and big pharmaceutical companies.[8] Yet in dentistry and medicine, as in many other occupations, those conflicts of interest are relatively easily defined: usually a personal (or direct) interest colliding with that of a client. In finance, the spectrum of conflicts seems more extensive, with a wider array of interested stakeholders. The following listing provides the most common of these conflicts of interest.

REMUNERATION AND INCENTIVES

When the modern corporation separated company management from ownership, the principal-agent (or agency) problem was born.[9] How can the principal (the shareholder-owner) be sure that the agent (the CEO-executive) pursues the owner's best interests? The solution involves a mix of control and alignment. Control or oversight of managers is vested in a board of directors supported by a legal framework. The board is given the power to hire and fire management, (dis)approve corporate strategy, and set managerial compensation. Alignment is achieved by designing incentives that match managerial goals with shareholder interests. Executive compensation should be structured so as to remove the agency conflict of interest.

Many financial institutions' managerial compensation packages are structured to incentivise executives to work towards share price (or profit) stretch targets, although in many this strategy is now under review. Most companies recognise good performance through salary increments, bonuses or promotion, incentives that tend to be a (small) fraction of the base salary. Not so in the finance sector, where managerial incentive components can be many multiples of the base salary. And it is not just at the CEO level where a comparison with remuneration at non-financial companies is most stark. The incentive component of salary has become increasingly large throughout the finance sector hierarchy.[10] Depending on the level of managerial seniority, those incentive components are generally based on specific key performance indicators, such as the company share price, operating profit, sales revenue, number of new customers and so on. It is this performance-based remuneration which has excessively raised finance sector incomes, causing significant ethical concerns around distributional justice and fairness. For the purposes of this chapter, we are mainly concerned with how the composition of remuneration creates a conflict of interest. (See Chapter 2 for further discussion of the ethics of compensation and incentives.)

Aidan Balnaves-James from the Seven Pillars Institute of Global Finance and Ethics wrote in 2015 that:

> Excessively high executive compensation linked to operational goals induces unnecessary risk-taking and increased probability of unethical, possibly unlawful behaviour ... Contemporary executive compensation packages generally comprise a combination of base salary, bonuses, restricted stock, stock options, perquisites and long-term incentive plans ... [These packages] attempt to converge the interests of executives with shareholders. [Yet] These compensation features act as incentives for executives to engage in potentially risky, profit-maximizing activities, which benefit shareholders [only] when ventures are successful.[11]

Executive stock options—an increasingly popular CEO performance pay component—increase in value when stock price volatility increases. This feature apparently aligns the CEO with shareholders' interests in considered risk-taking. However, when confronted with difficult market conditions (and profits are down), option compensation would encourage the executive to significantly increase risk-taking—exactly at a time when a more conservative approach might be called for. The value of stock options does not discriminate between 'good' and 'bad' volatility, but shareholders do!

Down the organisational hierarchy, bonus payments often form the major component of finance sector salaries. The bonus pool tends to depend on the sales revenue generated by a division. Not only does that create a strong conflict of interest regarding clients, it also creates a conflict of interest with other divisions (and by extension, with the company's best interests).

In the aftermath of the 2007–08 global financial crisis, some governments (such as that of the United States) imposed conditions on CEO pay in the institutions they had to bail out. The public outcry over the subsequent remuneration packages and generous severance pay deals suggested that this was not terribly effective. The school of thought that direct salary regulations may reduce the supply of talented individuals is still a mainstream one among the institutional investors who dominate the share ownership of those companies, which guarantees the approval of remuneration proposals at annual general meetings. In any case, the outcry seems to focus more on unethical excess than on removing misaligned interests.

Rather than relying on direct salary intervention by governments or their regulators, a 2009 inquiry by Australia's Productivity Commission proposed a focus on the remuneration role of the board of directors:

> Instead, the corporate governance framework should be strengthened by:
> - removing conflicts of interest, through independent remuneration committees and improved processes for use of remuneration consultants
> - promoting board accountability and shareholder engagement, through enhanced pay disclosure and strengthening the

consequences for those boards that are unresponsive to
shareholders' 'say on pay'.[12]

CORPORATE ADVISORY—BALANCING CLIENTS' INTERESTS

All too often, investment banks face the prospect of impersonal
conflicts of interest when dealing with 'connected' clients. Takeovers
and mergers—where the investment bank has a fiduciary relationship
with bidder and target—create the conditions for an actual conflict
when the two corporate clients have clearly diverging interests. In
some cases, the investment bank's own interests in the transaction may
further complicate the problem.

Consider the 2012 case of Goldman Sachs acting simultaneously for
two energy company clients engaged in a corporate takeover. The multinational financial institution also held a personal stake in the transaction. Reuters' reporters Michael Erman and Jessica Dye explained:

> Goldman Sachs was not paid a $20 million fee it billed for advising
> El Paso Corp on its more than $20 billion sale to Kinder Morgan Inc
> after the investment bank was accused of a conflict of interest in the
> sale. El Paso shareholders sued Kinder Morgan, alleging that the sale
> was tainted by Goldman's involvement with both energy companies.
> While it was advising El Paso, Goldman had a multibillion-dollar stake
> in the acquirer and its top energy banker held a $340 000 personal
> stake in Kinder Morgan.[13]

As investment banks have myriad client relationships with corporations competing within the same industries, and also run proprietary
services, actual conflicts of interest may be hard to avoid and therefore can be difficult to prosecute. Joyce Moullakis of the *Australian
Financial Review* reported on one such instance late in 2011:

> One of the most high-profile conflict of interest actions in Australia
> did … result in a loss for ASIC. In its case against Citigroup Global
> Markets Australia in 2007, the regulator had claimed that Citigroup
> was conflicted as the firm was conducting proprietary trading in
> shares related to companies involved in a takeover, while it was also
> advising suitor Toll Holdings on the transaction. It was found that

the relationship between the investment bank and the client was not fiduciary in character.[14]

AFFILIATED ANALYSTS

Sell-side analysts probably attract the most attention around poorly handled conflicts of interest in finance. A sell-side analyst (or equity analyst) writes research reports on the valuation of companies, and makes buy/sell/hold recommendations to the brokerage clients of a financial institution. Conglomerate financial institutions provide brokerage alongside their investment banking services. The investment bank advises corporate clients on IPOs and rights issues, and charges those clients commissions for successfully raising funds. To do this effectively, they need to have a brokerage operation to sell the securities. The bank's brokerage (and therefore the corporate client) stands to gain from favourable analyst recommendations. That means pressure on the analyst, possibly leading to an upwardly biased valuation. As equity analyst compensation is often tied to stock and investment banking results, actual conflicts of interest seem likely. The 2003 *Report on Analyst Conflict of Interest* by the International Organization of Securities Commissions said that 'the integrity of an analyst's research can only be achieved if situations of potential conflicts of interest are avoided as much as possible and, if not avoidable, properly managed and disclosed to investors'.[15]

In late 2015, Tim Stewart of InvestorDaily reported on the role of a corporate adviser in the privatisation of New South Wales' public electricity assets, which illustrates the issue of directed research. According to the report, UBS, the corporate adviser on the sale, allegedly changed its research report to align with its investment banking aspirations for a successful sale. The Australian Securities & Investments Commission (ASIC) agreed there was an issue, saying that it 'was concerned that UBS Securities' control framework relating to its research function, and its compliance with that framework, at the relevant times was not adequate for an investment bank of UBS's size and complexity. UBS Securities has acknowledged these concerns'. Stewart then wrote:

> The measures UBS is taking include the appointment of additional supervisory roles at UBS Securities' research department; the

appointment of an additional 'compliance resource'; the establishment of a research executive committee; improved training for UBS staff; and the publication of guidance for analysts regarding sensitive information. UBS Securities has also appointed an independent expert to review the implementation of the remedial measures.[16]

Buy-side analysts, who work for institutional investors, seem less exposed to accusations of bias. The key difference is that buy-side research is for internal use only. Unlike the blanket recommendations made by the sell-side analyst, the buy-side analyst works for only a single client: their employer. Buy-side analysts advise their employers on which securities to buy/sell/hold, and generate revenue when they make good calls. Their interest is to provide an objective valuation, directly aligned with their institutional employer's interests.

Independent analysts' interests are also aligned with their clients, as their compensation will depend to some extent on the quality of the analysis. Objective valuations build trust and are more likely to generate repeat business. Any incentive the analyst has to be biased will be offset by reputational and legal considerations favouring objective analysis. Increased use of peer group evaluation and an aspiration to be listed in analyst rankings (as conducted by *Institutional Investor* magazine, for example) also diminish a possible bias.

Since the spate of allegations of biased sell-side analyses in the late 1990s (focused on analysts covering worthless technology companies prior to the dotcom crash) and early 2000s (analysts covering the energy company Enron, which perpetrated a massive accounting fraud), governments and their regulators have attempted to put a halt to this systemic conflict of interest.[17] The persistently positive recommendations of poorly performing shares with few prospects by the world's leading financial institutions caught investors and regulators off guard. The lack of objective independent research caused the inevitable value correction to be sharper and deeper, with repercussions beyond the demise of the dotcom stocks, extending to an economic recession.

The US regulatory response included the 2003 Global Analyst Research Settlement, which mandated Chinese walls between research and investment banking, and enforced the use of independent analyst services. A 2017 study by professors of finance Shane Corwin, Stephannie Larocque and Mike Stegemoller found that the global settlement effectively reduced the affiliated analyst bias for the (small) group of banks covered by the settlement.[18] However, they also found that this positive impact of managing conflict of interest did not extend to the other banks that were not part of the settlement.

In 2009, Rosalyn Retkwa of *Institutional Investor* magazine discussed how the 2003 agreement between ten prominent Wall Street institutions and US regulators settled the allegations of undue influence exerted on sell-side research analysts to provide positive reports on IPOs managed by their investment banking divisions. According to Retkwa, among other terms, the agreement required brokers to physically separate their research and investment banking operations, and to buy research from at least three independent providers, so that customers would have access to non-proprietary research.[19]

By the time this global settlement expired in 2009, the finance landscape had changed, with online and internet-based brokerage services proliferating and competing with in-bank brokerages. These new technology-driven services specialised in executing trades, while their institutional investor clients obtained independent valuations from an increasingly competitive market for independent research. This unbundling of services has been particularly effective in the United Kingdom and continental Europe, not least due to the Markets in Financial Instruments Directive (MiFID II) regulations that are expected to take full effect in 2018. The European Securities and Markets Authority is behind the introduction of MiFID II, which includes regulations on the conduct of business and organisational requirements for investment companies.

The European regulations, as with similar US and Australian protocols, aim to remove or at least manage the inherent affiliated analyst conflicts of interest, including the following:

- *No promises of favourable research* prohibits analysts from offering a favourable rating to attract investment banking business. Specifically, it imposes *quiet periods* that prohibit banks acting as the manager of a securities offering from issuing an analyst report within forty days of the offering.
- *Limitations on relationships and communications* prohibit analysts from being supervised by the investment banking division. Beyond supervision, the investment bankers cannot discuss research with the analysts prior to distribution of the

research unless monitored by the legal/compliance department. Similarly, analysts are prohibited from sharing draft research reports with the companies they analyse (beyond fact-checking as approved by the legal/compliance department).

- *Analyst compensation and firm compensation* prohibits the linking of analyst compensation to specific investment banking transactions. Any general link between analyst compensation and investment banking revenue requires full disclosure.[20]

An opinion piece in *The Economist* magazine in 2014 suggested that the combined impact of the regulations in the United Kingdom had depleted the ranks of bank research analysts, arguably leading to a less informed and therefore less efficient financial market.[21] Of course, finance academics would argue that removing bias is more important than less volatility. There is also a suggestion that research will increasingly shift to the buy-side and independent analysts, making it either inaccessible or expensive to retail investors. That said, the sell-side research was never really free, and it seems preferable to pay for objective valuations rather than incur the cost of biased valuations.

The regulations also include *Personal trading restrictions and disclosure of financial interest*, which prohibits analysts (and their relatives) from investing in a covered company prior to a security offering. Specifically, analysts face a 'blackout period' regarding personal trading over a period of thirty days prior to and five days after research report publication, and they are expressly prohibited from trading against recent recommendations. In addition, any shares held in recommended companies require full disclosure of ownership.

HANDLING CONFIDENTIAL INFORMATION AND INSIDER TRADING

Employees' personal trading activity can be a major concern for a bank's legal/compliance department when managing and overseeing their access to material non-public information on client companies. Bank codes of conduct commonly require employees to respect the confidentiality of information obtained in the course of their employment. This includes market-sensitive (material) information regarding the investment value of a corporate client. Using material information for personal benefit would clearly be a violation of such codes.

Information is deemed material if its disclosure would likely have an impact on the price of a security, or if reasonable (rational) investors would want to know the information before making an investment decision. Materiality depends on the specificity of the information (establishing a clear link with a company's value), the extent to which it is different from public information, the nature of the information, and the reliability of the information. A (non-exhaustive) listing of typical material information that is likely to pass (more or less routinely) through a company's corporate banker, before it becomes public knowledge, would include:

- earnings announcements
- mergers, acquisitions, tender offers and joint ventures
- changes in assets
- innovative products, processes and discoveries
- new licences, patents, trademarks or regulatory approval/ rejection of a product
- developments regarding customers or suppliers
- changes in management
- loans, bonds and equity issues
- bankruptcies and bad debts
- significant legal disputes
- orders for large trades before execution.

Securities regulators worldwide prohibit selective disclosure, in particular to analysts. In the United States, Regulation Fair Disclosure, which was developed by the U.S. Securities and Exchange Commission (SEC), came into effect in August 2000. The regulation mandates that all public companies must disclose material information to all investors simultaneously. This stopped the earlier practice of pre-release equity analyst briefings. Of course, it is nearly impossible to ensure that *all* material information is made public at the same time, as it is first raised with (or becomes known to) the corporate banker. This is particularly relevant for a corporate bank that is engaged in advisory (or negotiating) services for the corporate client.

In citing a substantive case of insider trading in 1995 based on material non-public information of corporate clients, Kenneth Gilpin of *The New York Times* suggested that this was not a rare occurrence: 'The indictments come at a time when insider trading violations, the province of Wall Street deal makers and speculators in the mid-1980s, are being brought with rising frequency against current or former corporate employees and advisers who have learned of pending mergers or acquisitions'.[22]

To prevent bank employees from using material information in their personal trading, banks should create appropriate information barriers or firewalls to limit access to confidential material information. Those barriers would need to be complemented by:

- the documentation of procedures to limit the flow of material information
- internal (cross-barrier) communication control through a legal clearance area
- a review of employee trading based on watch/restricted/rumour lists of shares
- an increased review or restriction of personal trading while an employee is in possession of material information.

Still, despite measures such as these, recent examples abound of financial institution employees prioritising their personal interests over the corporate client's interests, the employer's interests and market integrity public interest—the alleged front-running of client orders over a five year period by a group of London bankers in the late 2000s is but one of these.[23] In a 2015 research paper, finance professors Henk Berkman, Paul D Koch and Joakim Westerholm presented evidence that employees of financial intermediaries seem to benefit from privileged access to material non-public information. Those employees are more active in their personal trading activity around major company-specific information events.[24]

An actual conflict of interest like this causes significant damage to the reputation of the employing financial institution in terms of loyalty and confidentiality. In addition, the corporate client would consider the abuse of its material information for personal benefit as theft. Yet the violation of market integrity is the most important consideration of the regulator in pursuing legal action against this type of insider trading. When fairness and transparency are violated through insider trading, trust in market integrity evaporates, undermining the financial system at large.

Sometimes the conflict of interest that causes insider trading extends beyond an employee's personal interests to the financial institution's interests. In some instances, material information may then also be obtained through abuse of position. An example of that scenario was the insider trading charge brought by the SEC in 2016 against a prominent hedge fund manager *and* his company. In its press release on the matter, the SEC stated:

> The SEC alleges that [Len] Cooperman generated substantial illicit profits by purchasing securities in Atlas Pipeline Partners (APL) in advance of the sale of its natural gas processing facility in Elk City, Oklahoma. Cooperman allegedly used his status as one of APL's largest shareholders to gain access to the executive and obtain confidential details about the sale of this substantial company asset. Cooperman and Omega Advisors allegedly accumulated APL securities despite explicitly agreeing not to use the material non-public information for trading purposes, and when APL publicly announced the asset sale its stock price jumped more than 31 per cent.
>
> ... 'We allege that hedge fund manager Cooperman, who as a large APL shareholder obtained access to confidential corporate information, abused that access by trading on this information', said Andrew J. Ceresney, Director of the SEC's Division of Enforcement. 'By doing so, he allegedly undermined the public confidence in the securities markets and took advantage of other investors who did not have this information.'[25]

A small minority argues that there is in fact a benefit to insider trading. By trading (early) on material information, price discovery is fast-tracked, improving the efficiency of the market. However, general opinion holds that the costs in terms of fairness, transparency, loyalty and confidentiality far outweigh a benefit that is better obtained through mechanisms such as Regulation Fair Disclosure.

MANIPULATING MARKETS ON FAKE NEWS

It would be difficult to argue that there are any benefits, beyond the perpetrator's personal gain, to be gained from market manipulation. Spreading misleading information that causes prices (and volumes) to divert from their true value can only make markets less efficient, give the wrong price signals, and lead to a misallocation of resources. Traditional market manipulation consisted of distorting demand for, or supply of, an asset. Commodity markets, due to their limited supply, provide many ill-fated opportunities; consider, for example, the copper derivatives manipulation that nearly defaulted Sumitomo Corporation.[26] Volume manipulation tends to be fairly 'visible' and eventually regulators step in to liquidate the manipulator's positions.

Modern-day market manipulation, which is similarly malicious, occurs through the spreading of rumours about imminent restructures, rating changes, or the financial distress of listed companies. The perpetrators of 'rumourtrage' effectively exploit the unchecked nature of social media. That said, while social media may have facilitated the planting of fake news in recent times, the practice has been documented for at least 200 years. In an article in mid-2015, Kathleen Pender of the *San Francisco Chronicle* put recent examples in a historical perspective, referring to the well-documented planned premature announcement of Napoleon's death on 21 February 1814, which temporarily sent London Stock Exchange prices soaring. While nowadays the perpetrators use more sophisticated communications technology, and verification of the news occurs more quickly, as Pender describes, the basics remain the same:

> The latest incident happened Tuesday morning, when an unknown perpetrator posted a story on a website closely resembling Bloomberg. com saying that Twitter had received a $31 billion takeover offer. The fake site had a different Web address, Bloomberg.market.com, than the authentic one. The story carried the by-line of a real Bloomberg reporter, albeit one who covers British banks, not social media. It also had misspelled words, including the name of former Twitter chief executive Dick Costolo. But it fooled enough people to cause a brief rise in Twitter's stock price before a Bloomberg spokesman, in a tweet, called the story a fake. Within 10 minutes, Twitter shares went up, then down, by 5 percent.[27]

However, it is not just the rogue trader, without fiduciary duties or market/public interest obligations, who engages in price manipulation. In the last decade, a number of global banks have manipulated the daily closing prices of financial instruments widely used as benchmarking or reference rates for loans, mortgages and deposits—in particular the key international interbank interest rates, including the London Interbank

Offered Rate (LIBOR) and the Euro Interbank Offered Rate (Euribor). This manipulation has had global repercussions for the markets concerned and, ultimately, for its perpetrators.

In mid-2015, Antoine Gara of forbes.com explained in some detail how one of the banks involved came to an agreement to settle the case with US and UK regulators:

> Deutsche Bank has disciplined or dismissed individuals involved in the trader misconduct, Fitschen and Jain [Deutsche Bank co-CEOs] said, and the bank has strengthened its control teams, and operating culture. 'This agreement marks another step in addressing the past and ensuring that the Bank earns back the trust of its clients, shareholders and society at large', they said.[28]

Again, individual bank employees may have engaged in what the industry refers to as 'rogue' trading. However, the number of banks (and their traders) involved suggests that the conflict of interest may have resided in the institution as well as with individual employees. Allegations against Barclays trying to manipulate LIBOR and Euribor interest rates first surfaced in 2005. And in 2013, Bloomberg News reported that a large number of global banks were suspected of having front-run clients and manipulated foreign exchange benchmark WM/Reuters rates for their own institutional interests.[29]

The significant systemic public detriment that is a consequence of manipulated prices makes this an alarming conflict of interest. The public, governments and regulators expect global banks to be the guardians of efficient, transparent and fair benchmark financial rates. When this expectation is not met, a loss of trust is inevitable.

COMMISSIONS AND FINANCIAL PLANNING

A 2011 ASIC report on a review of financial advice industry practice investigated the remuneration arrangements in Australia's financial services licensees, and concluded that these arrangements created significant conflicts of interest.[30]

Financial advisers perform two services:

1. They provide advice and make recommendations.
2. They sell and distribute financial products.

The provision of financial advice is competitive and relatively inexpensive, therefore it is difficult to make this a financially viable business. This may explain why the area of financial advice has become sales-oriented. The ASIC report indicated that more than half of the remuneration of financial advisers was generated by ongoing commissions, while close to 90 per cent of their remuneration was paid for by asset providers. Only 5 per cent was paid by clients as a fee for advice. Product sales volume, then, is overwhelmingly the key driver of the financial advice sector's revenue. So how likely does it seem that financial advisers are prioritising the interests of their clients over their personal and asset providers' interests?

It is no secret that financial advisers routinely recommend 'related party' products, which are tied to their own compensation. Since consumers are 'sticky' (they rarely switch advisers), ongoing commissions provide a guaranteed steady income stream without the adviser having to provide additional advice. The commissions also create an incentive for advisers to promote investment strategies rather than recommend other (prudential) options such as paying off an existing loan or credit card.

ASIC, as Australia's financial services regulator, has acknowledged a need for greater powers to intervene in finance advice sector pay structures, to remove incentives that lead to inappropriate product advice. Clancy Yeates of *The Age* recently reported that the watchdog

> is also seeking the power to ban certain types of pay structures that are clearly against the interests of customers, such as certain types of commissions ... ASIC's push for greater intervention powers comes as the banking industry is pledging to overhaul how it pays frontline staff, by reducing sales targets linked to bonuses, and cutting commissions paid to mortgage brokers.[31]

In 2010, the Australian Government first proposed the Future of Financial Advice (FOFA) reforms which significantly restrict the use of commissions.[32] This proposal generated interesting discussions between proponents of commissions and those who wanted them abolished. The proponents stressed FOFA's impact on the cost of advice, particularly regarding clients who could hardly afford it. The opponents, on the other hand, stressed the cost implied by the inevitable conflict of interest, a cost that would also be borne disproportionately by low-income clients. FOFA was eventually legislated in 2016 in the *Corporations Amendment (Financial Advise Measures) Act*, stressing clients' best interest duty, and a ban on conflicted remuneration—phasing out commissions. FOFA became mandatory on 1 July 2013.

Not all financial advisers spoke out against the new regulations. In an *Australian Financial Review* interview, the CEO of the financial advisory company Findex, Spiro Paule, said he understood the conflict of interest and could see the need for regulation:

> Findex boss Spiro Paule has banned his advisers from gleaning commissions, scrapping all commissions from July 1. 'I got my start thanks to those high upfront commissions, but I have always found it a very flawed system', Mr Paule said. This belief prompted Mr Paule to go a step further than new government reforms to cap hefty upfront commissions on life insurance products at 60 per cent of the premium in the first year of the policy.
>
> Mr Paule said he believed the industry was 'caught off guard' when the independent report it commissioned former Suncorp executive and Australian Prudential Regulation Authority member John Trowbridge to produce, in response to a damning Australian Securities and Investments Commission review, came down strongly in favour of limiting high upfront commissions.[33]

RATING AGENCIES

During the 2007–08 global financial crisis, rating agencies were caught in the spotlight of a destructive conflict of interest. On earlier occasions, rating agencies had been accused of lagging behind, rather than anticipating, changes in credit ratings. In their defence, the agencies argued that there was a significant cost to shareholders and other stakeholders when the change turned out to be wrong. This was the classic trade-off between two types of errors: type 1—predicting a change when it was not warranted; and type 2—predicting no change when it was warranted. In some cases, the rating agencies missed the clear signals altogether, or were slow to act on them; Enron is a good example.[34] But these specific cases were attributed mostly to a lack of professional competence, an inability to detect fraud through complexity.

What was mostly missed was the inherent conflict of interest whereby rating agencies relied on the revenue generated by repeat business from the companies they rated. The market for ratings is not particularly competitive, with Standard & Poor's, Moody's and Fitch accounting for 95 per cent of market share. This should diminish undue client influence on a rating agency. Nonetheless, a favourable rating is much more likely to please the company that's paying the agency's bills. It almost goes unnoticed when ratings are overly optimistic in a booming economy, but it is much harder to hide optimism bias when many companies do not perform or collapse simultaneously. This is exactly what happened in 2007–08, and it was possibly compounded by professional incompetence. The rating agencies were unable to grasp the extraordinary credit risk hidden in complicated mortgage-backed securities and collateralised debt obligations. They shared this lack of understanding with the uninformed investors, but unfortunately the latter relied on the agencies to signal poor creditworthiness.

Credit rating agencies do not only get paid for their rating services by the companies they rate. They also derive significant revenue from additional consulting services. In some cases, the rating agency may even design a new structured debt security for its client, whose creditworthiness it then goes on to rate. A 2016 study by professors of finance at the Stockholm School of Economics, Ramin Baghai and Bo Becker, showed a positive rating bias for Indian companies that also hired their rating agencies for other services, even though these companies tended to have higher default rates.[35] The researchers also found that the more money paid for other services, the larger the bias. To indicate how big these two revenue carrots can be, finance professors Stephen Cecchetti and Kermit Schoenholtz wrote on their website: 'In 2015, Moody's reported $2.3 billion in ratings-related revenues for Moody's Investor Services, and an additional $1.2 billion from other services from Moody's Analytics'.[36]

How to break this revenue dependency cycle? Regulators could mandate ratings at a fixed fee. Alternatively, they could impose the cost of rating on the investors who rely on the service. Additionally, rating agencies could be forced to separate their consulting services from their rating service; for example, through only consulting for clients who are not also using their rating service. However, the global nature of the rating companies would make these changes difficult to implement effectively.

The rating agencies admitted that some ratings were inaccurate in the lead-up to the global financial crisis, but then blamed the information they were provided. Floyd Norris of *The New York Times* reported on Moody's explanation:

> The chief executive of Moody's conceded on Friday that his agency had made significant mistakes in the rating of structured finance products, but added that the agency had been deceived by people who put together the products ... He said that one reason for the failure was that the 'information quality' given to Moody's, 'both the completeness and veracity, was deteriorating' as the subprime mortgage market grew.
>
> [The chief executive] vigorously defended Moody's, saying its work was 'not in some way corrupted by the business model'. He said there would be conflicts no matter who paid the fees, suggesting that a major investor paying Moody's might also put pressure on it to give high ratings to securities the investor already owned. That drew a strong response from the governor of the Mexican central bank: 'It is stretching the imagination to suggest that the conflict of interest would be comparable if you were being paid by the buyers'.[37]

MANAGING CONFLICTS OF INTEREST

Although conflicts may be difficult to avoid in diversified conglomerate financial institutions, Brian Hartzer, CEO of Westpac Banking Corporation, recently acknowledged in an *Age* interview the importance of dealing with those conflicts: 'The issue is not about having conflicts of interest ... it's all about how you manage those conflicts of interest'. Hartzer went on to say that his bank spent about A$300 million a year on compliance and he expected that figure to drop.[38]

Once a potential conflict of interest has been identified, what should be done next? The minimum regulatory or legal requirement would be *disclosure* of the conflict. Transparency would allow the conflicted parties to discount the bias in advice, or to disengage altogether. In general, more information provides for better decision-making. Yet, in a 2011 study, professors of management George Loewenstein, Daylian Cain and Sunita Sah suggested that disclosure might have a perverse impact: 'Disclosure introduces a possible rationalization for unethical behaviour: a person who has received disclosure should, perhaps, expect bias'.[39] Hence, disclosure becomes a moral licence to do the wrong thing. Consider a sell-side analyst disclosing a conflict of interest to a client. A rational client will discount the perceived bias of the advice accordingly. Having 'unburdened' themselves, the analyst can now opt to consciously be biased in their advice to an even greater extent than before—this is known as strategic exaggeration. The analyst probably knows how difficult it would be for the client to 'discount' the biased advice, particularly in a market where sell-side analysts dominate.

The disclosure of a conflict is normally perceived as a warning: handle with care. It diminishes the level of trust placed in the conflicted party. It is perhaps surprising to discover, then, that disclosure can in fact increase (misplaced) trust, as it is often seen as a signal of honesty (doing the right thing) or a signal of connectedness/reputation. Better-connected corporate advisers are bound to have more conflicts of interest as their reputations put them in high demand. That advantage trumps any disadvantage in the queue of declining interests. Consider the corporate adviser involved in the merger of two clients. While one client's interests may clearly be favoured, the other client could be inclined to stay with the same adviser as the ultimate outcome may still dominate any deal brokered by a corporate adviser of lesser repute.

From the above, it is clear that mandating disclosure is not sufficient. What would make disclosure effective, and even ethical? Disclosure should be relevant and complete, without too much detail and excessive information. In its 2015 report *Too Long; Didn't Read*, the Insurance Council of Australia indicated that increasingly complex and voluminous product disclosure statements in fact diminish the likelihood that the affected parties notice and pay attention.[40] A good starting point therefore would be to not just disclose the existence of a conflict of interest, but also its possible consequences. That would allow the disadvantaged party to better discount any biased advice, or to assess the extent of the disadvantage. Ideally, disclosure would then also include reference to independent advice for benchmarking. And it should be timely, allowing for a cooling-off period to give the affected parties time to distil the information before deciding either to continue or disengage.

As suggested for effective disclosure, reference to independent (unconflicted) advice may restore trust that a potential conflict does not automatically become an actual conflict. A declaration of *objectivity* in research, analysis, advice, trading and governance should signal the absence of bias or perceived disadvantage. Whether that signal is considered trustworthy will depend on reputation, third-party verification, or independent advice.

The simplest way to manage a conflict of interest is to *avoid* it. At its extreme, that would require the avoidance of any potential conflict of interest, yet the consolidated nature of financial service provision makes that almost impossible. We say 'almost' because, as Chapter 6 suggests, 'alternative' finance does seem to unwind the conglomerate service providers, with fintech (financial technology) operators carving out a place for niche or boutique financial services. These enjoy a major advantage due to their ability to effectively avoid conflicts of interest. Even then it may be difficult to anticipate or identify potential conflicts of interest before they arise. A moderate form of avoidance would be to prevent potential conflicts of interest from turning into actual conflicts. Whenever a conflict 'switches on', the conflicted finance professional is recused from the interaction/transaction. However, while that may sound straightforward, it ignores the employee's duty to the employer, and it denies the affected parties (customers) the opportunity to benefit from the professional's expertise.

The codes of conduct and compliance procedures of (most) financial institutions routinely comprise *policies and rules* that manage the most common conflicts of interest. Such codes and procedures set priorities for competing interests, require regular declarations of potential conflicts of interest, require employees to avoid acquiring adverse interests, curtail employees' personal trading activities, maintain 'quiet periods' during corporate restructures, and deal with material and confidential information, among many other institution-specific constraints. Yet despite the fact that these policies are made publicly available on corporate websites, many customers are still unaware of the various ways in which banks internally manage conflicts of interest. Of course, having policies, regulations and rules in place does not necessarily guarantee adherence. They should be complemented by compliance, oversight, audits and, most importantly, a commitment to high ethical standards. Without these, the rules are just words on paper.

In a 2003 speech to the US Securities Traders Association, SEC commissioner Cynthia Glassman said:

> The director of [the SEC] Enforcement Division recently challenged financial services firms to conduct systematic, top-to-bottom reviews of their business operations to identify conflicts of interest, disclose them and attempt to minimize their potentially harmful consequences ... This kind of preventive maintenance is not just a way of instilling a culture of compliance in your firms, but is also prudent business practice.[41]

Some financial institutions have opted for *independent judgement*, usually by establishing an independent advisory board as a subcommittee of the board of directors, chaired by one of its independent non-executive members. Alternatively, if independent judgement is truly kept at arm's-length, then it may take the form of an ad-hoc advisory committee consisting of academic and/or legal experts who act as consultants.

All of the above measures serve to mitigate the impact of actual conflicts of interest. When they are found wanting, governments and the relevant regulators have legislated/regulated for *structural change*. In 2006, ASIC deputy chairman Jeremy Cooper proposed a number of structural reforms, though they fell short of reintroducing a Glass-Steagall type separation of financial services (named after the 1933 US banking Act which, in response to the Depression, separated commercial from investment banking activities). The suggested reforms included:

- severing the link between analyst compensation and investment banking revenue
- prohibiting investment banking input in analyst compensation
- establishing a review committee to vet analyst research recommendations
- disclosing in research reports whether an analyst has received compensation from covered companies.[42]

In section 912A(1)(aa) of the *Corporations Act 2005*, the Australian Government mandated the obligation on the entire financial services sector to 'have adequate arrangements for managing conflicts of interest'. Responsibility for the oversight of regulated financial service entities and their compliance with the *Corporations Act* has fallen to Australia's securities regulator, ASIC.

Having adequate arrangements is not yet that prescriptive. Yet it is worth noting that no such requirement for comprehensive conflict of interest management exists in the United Kingdom or the United States as at late 2017. Many of Australia's banks have put detailed management plans in place, though, and made them publicly available. As an example, consider the Commonwealth Bank's 2017 conflict of interest policy as it relates to institutional research:

- Research staff reporting lines are structured to remove or significantly limit an actual or potential conflict of interest.
- No research staff report to client, trading or transactional areas, whose interests or functions may conflict with the research. These areas are also not involved in the determination of salary or bonuses, or in the content of their research.
- Where research staff assist product or transaction teams, this is controlled by strict Chinese Wall procedures.
- Staff may not receive gifts or inducements.
- Research staff make disclosures of personal interests.
- Staff cannot hold stock in the sector they cover; their trading is strictly controlled, and subject to specific restrictions whenever they are preparing research, or before company results presentations.
- The trading of all staff is subjected to a restricted list maintained by Compliance.
- Draft Research Reports are not provided to or reviewed by non-research personnel, although Research Analysts are permitted to check individual facts with companies before publication (without communicating the recommendations or opinions contained in the report).
- We do not provide recommendations on our own company or its products.
- There are strict barriers to prevent analysts having access to non-public information.
- Research declares when members of the CBA Group own more than 1% of any company which is the subject of research.

- We declare when members of the CBA Group have provided material non-research services to subject companies in the past 12 months.
- Non-research staff are prohibited from directing a research analyst to publish a Research Report and shall not direct the views and opinions expressed in a Research Report produced by Research.[43]

This is a comprehensive code of conduct, similar to those invoked by the Commonwealth Bank's competitor financial institutions. Of course, the implementation and cultural adoption of the code will ultimately determine whether trust is (re-)established.

CONCLUSION

Conflicts of interest, which undermine trust, are a continuing problem for the finance sector. Significant improvements in disclosure ironically have probably done more harm than good in exposing the extent of the problem. Disclosure statements have been implemented routinely but seem to have missed the mark in repairing trust. If the finance sector is to rebuild that trust, it will have to more actively manage, if not altogether avoid, conflicts. The above listed recommendations make sense and most are easy to implement, at least for individual conflicts of interest. Perhaps a better illustration and explanation of the economic and ethical cost of actual conflicts will make it more likely that those recommendations are in fact implemented and embraced by (rather than forced upon) the finance professional.

Maybe the institutional conflicts of interest are just too hard to avoid or manage. The successful appearance of small, niche financial operators and platforms avoids some of the pitfalls of built-in conflicts of interest in large, diversified conglomerate financial institutions. Merger and takeover panels (regulators) typically test whether proposed mergers/takeovers have anticompetitive consequences. In reaching a decision to approve or deny a corporate restructure, it may be worthwhile to also consider the appearance of and increase in (unmanageable) conflicts of interest.

6

ONE STEP AHEAD

Evolving Challenges

Paul Kofman

Futurists tell us we are on the brink of a fourth industrial revolution. This one is all about the digital and technological disruption of how we used to do things. Previous industrial revolutions saw many blue-collar manufacturing jobs replaced by machines, or disappear overseas to low-labour-cost countries. Developed economies like Australia successfully transitioned their labour force to white-collar service jobs. Now these jobs are themselves under threat, and the financial services sector is not immune. Many transactional services are moving online, or are being replaced by offshore call centres and, increasingly, by virtual services—known as robots or artificial intelligence systems. Yet the finance sector has also embraced and thrived on the opportunities created by digital disruption. The traditional banking sector in particular is constantly challenged by new, nimble and highly competitive operators, and must either change the tune of its service provision or face commercial oblivion.

In 2015, Michael Bennet of *The Australian* vividly described the new battleground for lending market share: 'the banks' battle for business customers is different to the past due to the horde of new fintechs—online small business lenders that have set up in the hope of capitalising on customer dissatisfaction with traditional lenders'.[1] Bennet noted that traditional banks are simply unable to effectively compete with the fintechs at the risk–return trade-off for small business lending.

The finance sector has in fact been remarkably resilient to change. In the ongoing capitalist battle of creative destruction, financial institutions seem to have had markedly greater longevity than manufacturing corporations. That could be explained by a sustained lack of competition, but it may also reflect an ability to adapt and adopt—adapt to new circumstances, such as the introduction of regulatory regimes such as Glass-Steagall or Sarbanes-Oxley, and adopt new technology like ATMs and internet banking, whenever and wherever they arise. There is no need for the financial establishment to significantly invest in research and development itself. Banking corporations have adopted a similar strategy to big pharmaceuticals: let independent niche operators innovate and create start-ups and ventures, and when they succeed, simply buy them. For example, the successful Australian upstarts specialising in low-cost mortgage lending (Aussie and RAMS) were eventually bought by the traditional banks (CBA and Westpac, respectively).

The sector's resilience is not just due to an ability to cope remarkably well with external pressure. Finance has become increasingly innovative and continuously reinvents itself to reduce the costs of regulation as well as the delivery of better products and services for customers. Regulators and legislators often struggle to keep pace with the latest developments in investment assets, financial advice and risk management. That often leaves new providers operating in a regulatory vacuum that only gets filled once things have gone terribly wrong, or once lobbying pressure by the sector itself becomes too strong to ignore. The cost of unregulated innovation on the public could be significant. Consider, for example, the fact that financial innovations like portfolio insurance and collateralised debt obligations contributed to the 1987 stock market crash and the 2007–08 global financial crisis, respectively. Rather than wait for legislation and regulation to catch up, we should therefore ask ourselves whether the ethics underpinning these innovations pass the morality test.

Digital technology will arguably improve market access for new (niche) financial institutions, as well as competition, and make markets and services more efficient. Robot trading and advice can significantly reduce fees, improve transparency, and make financial services more accessible. There is even a suggestion that robot finance will democratise the sector and lead to a more just and fair financial system for all. Human foibles and manifestations of conflicts of interest can simply be switched off. Taking out human interaction could transform a possibly immoral finance sector to an entirely amoral one where moral considerations simply have no role to play.

Unfortunately, this dehumanisation of finance raises its own ethical concerns. As finance sector legislation/regulation often significantly lags developments and practices, how can we be sure that financial entrepreneurs even consider the ethical implications of their new business models? After all, financial institutions often innovate to reduce the cost of regulation on conducting financial transactions. As many pieces of financial regulation have served to protect and entrench the market power of the incumbent banking sector, there may be a competitive-improvement argument that justifies the avoidance of regulation. Larry D Wall, executive director of the Center for Financial Innovation and Stability at the Federal Reserve Bank of Atlanta, suggested in 2014 that regulatory limits on the locations of bank offices and on competition between commercial and investment banks were anticompetitive regulatory examples.[2] However, if those regulations were put in place to protect vulnerable and informationally disadvantaged customers, then regulatory avoidance would be considered unethical.

Jessica Ellerm, writing on the website of BankNXT in 2016, identified the dehumanisation of finance as a major ethical shortcoming of fintech: 'To re-humanise our thinking, fintechs and banks can start to challenge the groupthink that suggests good, impartial and professional decision-making is without emotion'.[3]

These concerns extend from breaches of client information privacy to, more generally, neglect of a duty to clients. Perhaps surprisingly, they seem to have increased with the introduction of digital technology service platforms. While the platforms are notionally neutral, they don't recognise a client's financial sophistication or lack thereof.

Technology is not the only disruptor in financial services. Following decades of deregulation and globalisation, there are signs that the public is no longer accepting the benefits of these movements prima facie. Anti-globalisation protests have spilled into the mainstream. A growing distrust of multinational corporations and organisations was vindicated by a series of financial crises in the 1990s, culminating in the 2007–08 global financial crisis. To the public, (inter)national regulators seemed increasingly ineffective in their supervisory duties and in holding their country's financial institutions to account. Instead, the cost of avoiding widespread bank failure, leading to a systemic crisis, was entirely borne by the taxpayer. While driven by many other factors, the June 2016 Brexit vote—whereby the British voted for their nation's exit from the European Union—at least partly reflected discontent with having lost control of the British economy to corporations that don't answer to national jurisdictions. So is Brexit the start of a reversal of globalisation? That's hard to imagine, as the cost of lower economic growth and prosperity would be significant. Yet Brexit does illustrate what happens if trust in crucial institutions disappears and people feel disenfranchised.

At the same time as Europe has struggled to keep its financial system intact, China has emerged as a new financial powerhouse, challenging the dominance of the Western finance model. The 1997 Asian financial crisis gave the world a glimpse of the growing importance of, and rapid developments in, Asia's financial system. While the crisis did highlight China's financial fragility, the tenacious defence of the Hong Kong (HK) dollar by the HK monetary authorities also showed its remarkable resilience and endless resources. Progressive reform and deregulation of the Chinese economy has prompted the emergence of Shanghai as a global financial centre. Chinese banks are now opening branches around the world, and the Shanghai Stock Exchange has opened up foreign investment opportunities. Led by China's economic growth, Asia has become a magnet for investment banks, hedge funds, insurance companies and venture capital.

But China's finance sector is not without its challenges. The country's financial system is struggling to keep up with its economic growth. It has spurred a vast shadow banking network, raised concerns about governance and market integrity, and is subject to often opaque and constantly in-flux regulations and at times poor consumer protections. Combine those 'immaturities' with exuberant return expectations and very high (occasionally extreme) market volatility, and ethical concerns arise. China's financial and economic reforms successfully eliminated extreme poverty and raised living standards, but they also created significant income inequality, raising questions of justice and fairness.

In addition to technological and international disruption, the finance sector is also coming to terms with social disruption. Despite global economic growth, increasing prosperity and an absolute reduction in extreme poverty, the benefits of access to the financial system are still proving elusive to hundreds of millions of very poor people mostly but not exclusively living in developing countries. They simply lack any access to the most basic financial services. The growth of social banking and microfinance may be the key to providing the so-called 'unbankables' with limited financial resources as a pathway to longer-term traditional banking services. But despite the socially positive intentions of microfinancing, its very success does raise ethical concerns.

INNOVATION—FINTECH AND P2P

The basic functions of financial institutions are much the same as they have been for hundreds of years: payment services, financial intermediation services, and risk-management services. Throughout its history, the finance sector has not been immune to disruption and innovation in these services. The pace of change, however, has picked up markedly in the last two decades. Being physically present at a stock exchange or bank was once necessary to participate in transactions and services—the relevant news and information only found a public audience once filtered through newspapers a day after a relevant event. If the material event occurred overseas, it could take weeks or months to become public knowledge. Then ticker tapes and Bloomberg screens made markets more transparent, allowing more efficient interactions and fast international communication, but only to those who had access to the expensive technology, like brokers and financial institutions. It was the internet that truly revolutionised public access to real-time financial transactions. From Akureyri in Iceland to Ushuaia in Argentina, you can now buy Greek Government bonds and hedge the coupons in euros to kronor or pesos at a click of your mouse.

This digital revolution is rapidly replacing physical markets and bank branches and employees with online platforms and smartphone technology. Even the world of financial advice, which is still clinging to face-to-face transactions, might well be replaced by robot advice in the near future. The platforms are cheap to develop, easy to implement, and effectively marketed. This creates an entirely new competitive landscape, with start-ups and small players specialising in specific services instantly becoming competitive entrants. Whereas regulators used to impose the same regimes on incumbents and newcomers, who were thereby disadvantaged, they now seem to provide regulatory exception to new initiatives. Public distrust of the finance sector has weakened the lobbying power of the incumbents and convinced the regulators to encourage innovation and competition by newcomers. The price paid, however, is possibly unchecked unethical behaviour by the innovators.

FINTECH

Fintech is the catch-all term for financial innovation driven by digital technology and automation. It has practically become a corporate sector in its own right, with its very own spin-offs like regtech (automation of regulatory compliance), insurtech (automation of underwriting) and wealthtech (exploitation of data analytics, automation of transactions and robot advice).[4] Martin Wolf, chief economics commentator at the *Financial Times*, suggested in 2016 that fintech had the potential to right some of the ethical wrongs in the finance sector:

> Today, banks and insurance companies are the core financial institutions ... Why might one hope that new financial technology, or 'Fintech' as it is known, will transform these businesses? The answer, especially for banking, is that they are currently not done very well. Banking seems inefficient, costly, riddled with conflicts of interest, prone to unethical behaviour, and, not least, able to generate huge crises.[5]

But of course, fintech is not imposed on the banks. The banks embrace the new technology because of the benefits it brings in raising revenue, cutting costs and servicing customers. It is the economic imperative that appears to take precedence in the banks' decision to adopt digital technology.

A 2015 report by KPMG, *Making Hong Kong a Fintech Centre*, illustrated how one traditional financial institution had already invested in digital technology:

Perhaps the biggest market for new FinTech products and processes will be the banks themselves. Goldman Sachs's CEO Lloyd Blankfein has repeatedly described Goldman as a tech company, an assertion backed up by the fact that his bank has more software engineers and programmers than Facebook—possibly twice as many.[6]

Internet and smartphone banking has clearly been embraced (and trusted) by the public. But it is not clear if all expressions of fintech (data analytics, robot advice and so on) will be accepted by the public as more trustworthy than the finance sector of old. There is a strong suspicion that data analytics—made possible by fintech—will target customers to generate additional sales, and older generations tend to distrust services dispensed by machines and their programmers.

DATA ANALYTICS

'Big data' that reveals all about our daily financial lives has well and truly arrived. In fact, it has been here for some time, but only now are data scientists able to utilise advanced computer hardware and design capable, user-friendly and informative algorithms to successfully explore the data for valuable commercial insights. Financial markets had a head start in this area, with high-frequency, transaction-level data becoming available from the late 1980s, when physical exchanges were first replaced by automated trading systems. Conglomerate banks have also been gathering ever-more-specific information on their customers' behaviour through their multiple business lines (loans, deposits, payments, insurance, investments and so on). Persuading those customers to use internet banking and online services provides even more insights into their financial lives. In recent times, the digitisation of all customer–bank interactions has made matching previously disconnected databases much easier, allowing the data analytics to reveal patterns that suggest targeted service provision.

In 2013, Mark Halverson of *Digitalist Magazine* discussed the sometimes not so subtle distinction between customer choice and customer manipulation:

> In the world that we live in, dramatic amounts of information can be used, processed, segmented and re-segmented. Propensity models can be created and then tested against a series of customer segments. However, because we're using big data to influence the kinds of

experiences we offer, and to elicit certain behavior, we could be headed down a slippery slope.[7]

Despite privacy concerns, possible violations to the duty to clients, or the abuse of (material) client information, regulators have yet to impose limits and/or restrictions on the use of big data analytics, although it is an area of much inquiry and discussion.

CROWDFUNDING AND P2P BANKING

State-owned telecommunications companies lost their monopolies when analog networks and landlines were overtaken by digital technology and mobile phones, and bank lending is now at risk of a similar erosion of market share. It has never been easier for new entrants to pick off profitable, easily accessible customers. Online platforms, social media and cheap online marketing allow for direct financial transactions—cutting out the intermediating financial institution—where a borrower applies for a loan funded by a crowd of investors.

Crowdfunding comes in many different forms but generally involves a specific (philanthropic or entrepreneurial) investment opportunity. It can be reward-based, equity-based or loan-based. A borrower submits a plan (purpose) and asks lenders to contribute, either without repayment (in lieu of social reward), in exchange for a stake in the venture (equity), or with interest payments. The investment opportunity remains open until the required amount has been funded. A small percentage fee is usually levied by the platform provider.

The rapid growth in disintermediated lending could be indicative of the lack of trust in traditional bank lending or, more likely, the unmet demand for small (unsecured) loans that banks do not want to or cannot provide for regulatory reasons. Other factors contributing to this growth are the significant bank fees for personal and small business loans, and the much better returns on crowdfunded loans. Of course, crowdfunding exposes investors to significant counterparty risks. After all, how can you be sure that the borrower is genuine and can be trusted to use the money for the stated social award, investment in an entrepreneurial start-up, or repayment of a loan for wedding celebrations? There is also little chance of legal recourse or settlement. That said, some of the crowdfunding platforms are aware of the need for reputation credentialing, much like eBay does.

In 2014, the UK-based *Ethical Consumer Magazine* highlighted the specific risks surrounding crowdfunding and how these could be tackled by the UK's Financial Conduct Authority:

> ... the current lack of standardised regulation across all crowdfunding platforms results in consumer protection issues such as fraud, and misleading advertising and advice. Some of these issues may be addressed when the Financial Conduct Authority (FCA) takes responsibility for the regulation of the [UK] consumer credit market in April 2014 ... the FCA will implement guidelines for loan-based and equity-based crowdfunding platforms. These regulations will essentially involve implementing safeguards to check whether investors are able to understand and bear the risks involved in investing money.[8]

Peer-to-peer (P2P) lending is in many ways similar to (loan-based) crowdfunding, although the matching of lenders to borrowers is different. When a borrower applies for a loan, the P2P 'manager' auctions the loan to a registered pool of possible investors who bid by submitting their expected interest rates. The loan is then awarded to the lowest bidder. The manager can also bid, using their insights into the other submitted bids as well as a better-informed insight into the creditworthiness of the borrower—which causes obvious potential conflicts of interest.

In P2P lending, as in crowdfunding, borrowers and lenders avoid bank intermediaries through direct finance using an online lending platform. At present, most P2P lending is for relatively small personal and business loans and is only making a minor dent in traditional bank lending. Nonetheless, P2P growth rates are outstripping bank lending growth rates. The banks are therefore taking notice, demanding that P2P should be properly regulated. In late 2016, Clancy Yeates of *The Age* quoted one Australian bank chief as follows: 'Former ANZ chief Mike Smith last year said regulators should be wary of new risks being introduced through disruptive changes such as peer-to-peer lending'.[9]

These online lending platforms are currently unregulated. That means, for example, that lenders/depositors have no recourse to government guarantees as extended to bank term deposits. At the same time, that risk is offset by a higher expected return and the absence of fees. As long as the conditions of depositing are transparent, and investors are fully informed of the risks, this does not necessarily cause an ethical concern.

Much like the regulated taxi industry's complaints about Uber, banks argue that the exemption of regulation creates an unfair competitive advantage for P2P lenders. According to Sarah Todd of the *Financial Times*, in 2014 some prominent financial institutions made their discontent very clear to their own employees: 'Ethics administrators at Wells Fargo decided to forbid staff from P2P lending after concluding "that for-profit peer-to-peer lending is a competitive activity that poses a conflict of interest"'.[10]

While complaints by the competition are rarely a sound motivation for a regulator to take action, there are certainly examples of unethical behaviour in the P2P lending market. Last year's experience of Lending Club, a major P2P lender, raised questions about a possible misrepresentation of both the investment opportunity—through misstating the quality of the loans—and investment performance. If true, both actions would likely violate the ethical duty to clients and at least cast a shadow over the P2P platform's professional competence in assessing borrowers' creditworthiness. Ian Salisbury of Time.com reported on the controversial funding of Lending Club's loans in the lead-up to the resignation of its CEO in 2016:

> The events at Lending Club have raised some eyebrows. After all, if the company is willing to sell mislabeled goods to one of its largest and most sophisticated clients, why should Joe Investor assume he'll be treated any better? 'It brings up issues of trust', [said] a stock analyst that follows the company. 'Small investors need to be sure they are receiving the loans they signed up for.'[11]

BLOCKCHAIN

Originally developed to execute cryptocurrency transactions (that is, bitcoins), the substantive innovation of blockchain is a digital distributed ledger in which transactions are recorded chronologically and publicly—eliminating the need for centralised settlement. Not only does this significantly speed up transactions, it also incurs much less cost and decreases settlement times. It has been suggested that the transparency of the system will also reduce the likelihood of fraud. What it does not achieve is a guarantee of centralised clearing, long held to be the effective elimination (or at least reduction) of counterparty credit risk. Maybe that is why this collaborative technology (sharing a common system) is so far only open to fully credentialed institutions, including banks, who use it for payment services. Further applications include linking institutional investors and investment markets, creating private markets; for example, Nasdaq's private market initiative. Again, access would be strictly vetted to only allow trusted participants.

An ethical concern of blockchain is the creation of exclusive markets, somewhat like dark pools in equity markets, whereby increasing portions of transactions are conducted outside public markets. Distorting price discovery and privileging certain customers over others results in actual conflicts of interest and unfair treatment of customers.

CONCLUSION

In its 2016 report *The Role of Financial Services in Society: Understanding the Impact of Technology-enabled Innovation on Financial Stability*, the World Economic Forum recommended that in the context of technological disruption, the financial services sector needed to be proactive in the following ways:

- engaging in a public debate on the ethical use of data
- identifying supervisory support to develop technology that enhances system stability
- monitoring and mitigating the risks from technology-enabled innovation
- setting industry standards for good conduct with technology-enabled innovation.[12]

Those risks and standards should most certainly cover the ethical conduct of the technology disruptors, and consider the ethical impact of the new technology.

BREXIT AND THE RISE OF CHINA

Two international developments stand out in terms of their potential to significantly shape the financial services landscape. The first is the threat of the disintegration of the European Union (EU) in the wake of Brexit. The crisis leading to Brexit was kickstarted by the bailout of the Greek Government and the near-defaults of various other Mediterranean countries, and European nations are now reconsidering the benefits of integration. In particular, EU member countries are assessing whether the supposed benefits of free trade and economic growth are still worth the relinquishment of national government powers to Brussels. When economies are growing, the benefits can outweigh the costs, but following the inevitable economic downturn, economic integration suddenly seems expensive. Hence, we are witnessing a possible reversal of decades-long international cooperation, and a reinstatement of trade barriers and other protectionist measures. After the public bore the cost of the global financial crisis, its trust in globally operating financial institutions eroded even further than already signalled by anti-globalisation protest movements. It is hardly surprising, therefore, that very few British voters (of those who voted in favour of exit) gave a second thought to the possible consequences a Brexit vote would have on the future of the City of London as a global financial centre.

Brexit was an expression of public discontent with supranational institutions—in this case, the European Commission and multinational corporations in general—not answering to national jurisdictions. This is a typical agency problem where the governance of public or private institutions is no longer responding to the stakeholders' interests and the governments/regulators are incapable of effective supervision.[13] That public sentiment probably first emerged from the anti-globalisation movement of the 1990s. Just when global business—with financial institutions in the lead—was cresting a wave of trade liberalisation, it forgot to convince the public that this was, in fact, a good thing. The protests focused on how globally operating financial institutions and multinational corporations apparently conducted business outside any regulatory or legislative framework, while fuelling unemployment, income inequality and environmental damage. Just as the violent protests petered out, the global financial crisis came crashing down to reinvigorate the public's distrust of finance. Public anger turned towards the financial (for causing it) and political (for not doing enough to stop it) establishments, and resulted in the 2011 Occupy Wall Street movement. Again the protests dissipated, but the mood lingered. While Brexit had many causes, among them was a build-up of distrust caused by both alleged and real unethical behaviour by financial institutions.

So what are the ethical implications of Brexit for the finance sector? A reversal of globalisation will return legislation and regulation to national jurisdictions. That is potentially confusing and costly to the banks and their customers. UK market participants predict the departure of international financial institutions and their employees (with Frankfurt a likely beneficiary), and Brexit could also cause a significant decline in financial services competition and the loss of a competent finance workforce. The resulting concentration of market power involving the leftover UK financial institutions, and the reduction in professional competence, could well challenge ethical behaviour.

The second international challenge is China asserting itself as an economic and financial powerhouse. The 1989 collapse of the Soviet Union and communist Eastern Europe created the conditions for Western financial institutions to move in and expand their operations. In doing so, they also expanded the Western-style financial system and the matching regulatory framework. In China, however, communism still prevails, and internal economic reforms have allowed the Chinese Government to develop and nurture its own financial institutions and maintain tight control over its financial system.

In many ways, these reforms have been very successful. State-owned commercial banks like Industrial and Commercial Bank of China, and China Construction Bank, are rapidly expanding their presence in the Asian region and beyond. At the same time, many international financial institutions have become attracted to the burgeoning market demand for financial services in China. Yet all that new activity has proved insufficient to meet the insatiable demand for business loans, and so non-bank entities—known as shadow banks—have filled this void. While China's central bank, the People's Bank of China, has acknowledged the many risks (including ethical ones) of shadow banking, the contribution of this unregulated sector to the country's economic growth is simply too important to force these non-banks into regulatory compliance. *Financial Times'* reporter Gabriel Wildau illustrated the dilemma in an article in early 2017:

> China's central bank has drafted new rules to tackle risks from shadow
> banking, in a tacit acknowledgment that a host of measures in recent
> years to control off balance sheet credit have failed to control its

risks. New credit hit a record high in January, mostly due to lending by non-bank institutions. UBS estimates that China's ratio of debt to gross domestic product hit 277 per cent at the end of 2016, up 133 percentage points since the global financial crisis. Non-bank lending has grown the fastest. Banks have worked with other financial institutions to shift loans off balance sheet, allowing them to evade credit quotas and capital adequacy requirements. Regulators have permitted the rise of shadow lending, which is necessary to generate the overall credit growth required to meet the government's ambitious yearly growth targets without overburdening bank balance sheets.[14]

In a 2015 paper, Douglas Elliott, Arthur Kroeber and Yu Qiao, research fellows at the Brookings-Tsinghua Centre in Beijing, described the appeal of shadow banking to the operators and their clients.[15] At the same time, these attractions are also shadow banking's core risks. They include the negatives of formal banking—constraints on bank lending, maintenance of a loan-to-deposit ratio, and the regulatory discouragement of particular industry lending—and the positives of shadow banking: lower capital/liquidity requirements and the avoidance of costly regulatory reserve requirements.

The challenge to the financial services sector beyond China is how to respond to similar shadow banking initiatives that are emerging in other countries. Australia's regulator recently flagged the risks of having its own share of shadow banking activity. Early in 2017, Su-Lin Tan of the *Australian Financial Review* described how these unregulated non-banks circumvent the tightening regulatory constraints on real estate investment loans extended by the regulated banks.[16] The significant economic externalities of the housing price bubble perpetuated by shadow banks raises serious ethical concerns.

REACHING OUT TO THE UNBANKABLES

Microfinance is sometimes held up as an example of the ethical con-science of finance. Dedicated microfinance student clubs illustrate the current generation of students' ambitions to do good with finance. What exactly is so appealing about it? A large proportion of the world's population has no access to the formal financial system. These so-called unbankables are at best at the mercy of the informal moneylenders, or simply lack any access to financing at all. Microcredit extends microloans to the poorest of society, often women, for the purpose of empowering them to start small businesses to help themselves and their families escape from entrenched poverty.

While perhaps not the first to recognise the opportunity, Muhammad Yunus' Grameen Bank, which was established in 1976, became the global template for microcredit provision that is funded and supported by local communities. Broad recognition of its potential only occurred when Yunus was awarded the Nobel peace prize in 2006. General discontent with traditional finance, and with global finance organisations like the International Monetary Fund and World Bank, further encouraged the favouring of microfinance initiatives as meaningful and ethical alternatives. Since then, microfinance has expanded significantly across the developing world, as well as reaching out to impoverished and low-income communities in developed economies.

Perhaps not surprisingly, as every new initiative has its detractors, criticisms of Grameen Bank soon started to surface, and more generally, complaints about the very concept of microfinance. These included allegations of fraud, loan sharking, excessive indebtedness, high rates of default resulting in suicides and the impact of communal pressure. The effectiveness of microfinance in fighting poverty was also questioned. Had good finance turned into bad finance?

In 2012, more bad news surfaced, as reported by Associated Press, regarding a number of very successful microfinance organisations:

> More than 200 poor, debt-ridden residents of Andhra Pradesh killed themselves in late 2010, according to media reports compiled by the government of the south Indian state. The state blamed microfinance companies—which give small loans intended to lift up the very poor—for fueling a frenzy of over-indebtedness and then pressuring borrowers so relentlessly that some took their own lives. The companies, including market leader SKS Microfinance, denied it.
>
> The deaths came after a period of hypergrowth leading up to the company's hugely successful August 2010 initial public offering. Originally developed as a nonprofit effort to lift society's most down-trodden, microfinance has increasingly become a for-profit enterprise that serves investors as well as the poor. As India's market leader, SKS has pioneered a business model that many others hoped to emulate.[17]

Underlying these allegations was a profound questioning of the intrinsic motivation of some of the lenders. Initially funded by local governments, community cooperatives and NGOs, these not-for-profit institutions soon hit capacity constraints when trying to expand their operations from a cottage industry to a regional, or even national, financing facility. The scaling up of activity became necessary to make a meaningful impact on national poverty alleviation. Yet doing so meant raising the necessary capital externally. Mutual funds and hedge funds, always looking for diversification and assets with new high-risk/high-return profiles, jumped at the opportunity.

Many hedge funds have a simple economic motivation: maximise the risk-adjusted return on investment for their investors. Of course, Grameen Bank and similar microfinance institutions also shared an economic objective, but it was tempered by a strong social and ethical objective. By accessing purely commercial capital, this was about to change. Effectively, the dilution of social capital changed these institutions from cooperative to corporate entities. That change cut the intricate ties between community-based lenders and borrowers, and removed much of the social interest and control that had previously existed.

So what to do? Avoid sources of funding if the lender's aspirations and incentives are not perfectly aligned with social interest? Cap loan sizes, and possibly exclude borrowers already in arrears from accessing further loans? Cap interest rates at socially acceptable levels? And what exactly is ethically acceptable? As it turns out, there is no easy answer—perceptions of what is right differ and depend on the ethical position. That is, a utilitarian ethics position would look favourably on the broader reach of microfinance funded by profit-oriented funding. A duty-based ethics position would seriously question whether extending loans to people with few prospects should ever be considered at profit-driven interest rates. And a virtue-based ethics position would possibly only ever consider the socially oriented funding of microfinance loan.

CONCLUSION

The finance sector is continuously evolving, but now more than ever before, traditional financial institutions are being challenged by the opportunities provided by digital technology, the rise of China's shadow banking, and the ethical shortcomings of globalisation. While it is tempting to conclude that fintech and alternative finance offers ethical improvements, there are also serious ethical concerns. Regulators cannot stand idly by while the trade-offs unfold. Instead, they need to be proactive and qualify those concerns against the benefits of increased competition.

Brexit provides a stark warning for the future of the financial sector. Without balancing the economic (profit) imperative exploiting a globalised market, with a social/ethical imperative, people lose trust in global institutions. The inevitable protectionist and nationalist backlash is not only bad for finance sector business, it is likely to diminish the efficiency and increase the cost of financial services, and weaken competition in the sector. It's a high price for losing trust in global finance.

7

TAKE THE PRESSURE DOWN
Ethics Informing Practice
Clare Payne

ETHICAL AWARENESS

To be ethically aware is to understand the motivations and biases that may influence our decisions and actively mitigate their impact. Individuals can develop ethical awareness through first understanding the various factors, such as self-interest, self-deception, bias and workplace culture, that impact decisions.

MORAL COMPASS

A moral compass refers to an inner sense that distinguishes what is right from what is wrong, operating as a personal guide akin to that of a compass used for navigation. Some prefer to use the term 'gut instinct' in relation to decision-making, with 'gut' referring to an instinctive feeling as opposed to a considered opinion or a position based on facts.

Nobel laureate Daniel Kahneman and psychologist Gary Klein explored the issue of whether we can actually rely on our gut in a 2009 *American Psychology* article, and again in an interview for *McKinsey Quarterly*. They concluded that we cannot prevent our gut instinct from influencing our judgements. However, it is possible to identify situations where we are likely to be biased and strengthen our decision-making processes to reduce risks and thus make better decisions.[1] Most importantly, people have the opportunity to 'calibrate' and refine their gut instincts. This can be done by moving beyond reliance on a moral compass, which may have been adopted without much thought, towards an 'ethical compass' that has been consciously adopted and developed.

SELF-INTEREST

Self-interest refers to a focus on the needs and desires of the self. Within the context of finance, references to self-interest tend to dwell on the decisions and actions that elicit financial gain for individuals and companies over the interests of customers and other stakeholders.

Those who have studied economics will be familiar with the theories of Adam Smith in relation to self-interest and competition in the market economy. Smith concluded that the best economic benefits for all can actually be achieved when individuals act in their own self-interest. His theory of the 'invisible hand' held that when people act in their own self-interest, then goods and services are created that benefit consumers and producers; the concept was first raised in Smith's work *The Theory of Moral Sentiment*.[2] Smith held that self-interest is arguably the single largest motivator of economic activity. In his book covering the subject, *The Wealth of Nations*, he said, 'It is not from the benevolence of the butcher, the brewer or the baker that we expect our dinner, but from their regard to their own interest'.[3]

Supreme Court justice Lucy McCallum, however, highlighted the ramifications of the unfettered pursuit of self-interest when sentencing Oliver Curtis for insider trading conspiracy in June 2016. *The Sydney Morning Herald* quoted her as saying of Curtis, 'While many people have spoken of his positive qualities in business and as a family man, he shows no sign of progression beyond the self-interested pursuit of material wealth which prompted his offending'.[4]

Despite many examples to the contrary, a number of academics and commentators have questioned this perception of individuals. Lynn Stout, distinguished professor of corporate and business law at Cornell Law School, holds that we have blinded ourselves to our own goodness, and highlights an abundance of data from psychology, law and other disciplines suggesting that people are in fact motivated by more than just self-interest. In her book titled *Cultivating Conscience: How Good Laws Make Good People*, Stout draws from social psychology, behavioural economics and evolutionary biology to demonstrate how social cues, such as instructions from authorities, ideas about other's selfishness and unselfishness, and beliefs about benefits to others, have a powerful role in triggering unselfish behaviour.[5]

SELF-DECEPTION AND MORAL FADING

In an attempt to understand unethical behaviour, the concepts of self-deception and moral fading have been explored. Self-deception allows one to behave in their self-interest while, at the same time, falsely believing their moral principles are being upheld. The result is that the ethical aspects of a decision can 'fade' into the background, with the moral implications of a decision or behaviour obscured.

John Knapp, founder of The Southern Institute for Business and Professional Ethics in Atlanta, Georgia, argued in 1999 that unethical corporate behaviour emerges when well-meaning individuals blind themselves to the moral dimensions of their activity. Knapp warned that this can inadvertently wreak havoc upon the public good. He went on to identify four categories of corporate self-deception:

1. tribalism—the belief that the company is always right
2. legalism—the inability to imagine moral obligations beyond the law
3. moral relativism—the excusing of unethical practices by viewing business as 'a game' and oneself as having 'a role'
4. scientism—the elevation of science, including management science, to a position of unquestioned authority.[6]

BIASES

Biases of which individuals may not even be fully aware can influence their decisions and actions. Bias is a prejudice in favour of or against a thing, person or group compared against another, usually in a way that's considered unfair. Biases may be held by an individual, group or institution, and can have negative or positive consequences.

Biases are commonly divided into two groups:

1. conscious bias, also known as explicit bias
2. unconscious bias, also known as implicit bias.

There is an increasing focus on understanding our unconscious biases, with some organisations offering training programs to draw attention to this influence. Unconscious biases commonly revolve around social stereotypes about certain groups of people that individuals form outside their own conscious awareness—it is important to note that everyone holds unconscious beliefs and these biases stem from our tendency to organise our social worlds by categorising.[7] Unconscious bias is more prevalent than conscious prejudice, and often is actually incompatible with one's conscious values. Certain scenarios can activate unconscious attitudes and beliefs; for example, biases may be more prevalent when multitasking or working under time pressure.

Research by Rebecca Dore, Kelly Hoffman and Angeline Lillard, published in a 2014 article in the *British Journal of Developmental Psychology*, indicated that unconscious biases develop at an early age, emerging during middle childhood and developing across the rest of childhood.[8] However, our biases are not permanent. In fact, psychology professor Nilanjana Dasgupta, in his 2013 journal article 'Implicit Attitudes and Beliefs Adapt to Situations: A Decade of Research on the Malleability of Implicit Prejudice, Stereotypes and the Self-Concept', wrote about how unconscious biases are malleable and steps can be taken to limit their impact on our thoughts and behaviours.[9]

Strategies that can be used to address unconscious bias include increased self-awareness, understanding the nature of bias, and engaging in opportunities to have discussions with others, particularly those from socially dissimilar groups.

WORK CULTURE

Work cultures are shaped by shared beliefs, expectations and meanings that then influence and guide the thinking and behaviours of the individuals that work within them. An organisation's culture can be its sustaining value, offering direction and stability during challenging times, or it can serve to constrain individuals within a common way of thinking and acting that may not be in the interests of the organisation. Some may claim 'That's the way things have always been done around here' as a way to explain their behaviour or guide others. Dr Simon

Longstaff of The Ethics Centre warns that such unthinking customs and practices should be considered the 'enemy of ethics'.

Ethical work cultures are instead the ones in which individuals are empowered and expected to act in ethically responsible ways even when the law or a company rule does not require it. Compliance with the law alone can be insufficient to guarantee ethical conduct, particularly given that the law can lag societal changes and financial innovation. The acceptance of voluntary ethical standards that may be above the legal minimum is a core component of a profession and an expectation of the professionals that practise within it.

Risk and compliance professionals are increasingly turning their interest and expertise to understanding and studying workplace cultures. This increased focus will undoubtedly provide much-needed insights and assist in painting a full picture of an organisation and its operations. In particular, it will present an opportunity for human resources professionals to be active in driving programs and initiatives based on evidence as well as comprehensive insights from across the organisation. While work culture historically has been considered the responsibility of human resources, it is clearly the responsibility of all individuals, especially managers and leaders.

THE INFLUENCE OF OUR ENVIRONMENT

In our personal and professional lives, environment plays a significant role in shaping our decisions and actions. It is well documented that work environments are a significant driver of behaviour, ethical or otherwise. A body of research originally co-developed in the 1970s by Gerald Salancik, an American organisational theorist and professor at Carnegie Mellon University in Pittsburgh, Pennsylvania, and Jeffrey Pfeffer, a professor of organisational behaviour at Stanford Graduate School of Business in California, concluded that individuals look for cues in their work environment in order to guide them on how to behave, particularly when facing ambiguous or uncertain situations.[10]

Despite evidence that the environment and context of decisions and behaviours matters and wields significant influence, explanations of unethical behaviour tend to focus on the individual. Within the finance sector, the analysis of fraudulent and unethical behaviour typically identifies 'bad apples' or 'rogues', the latter term somewhat synonymous with 'trader'. This use of words as labels seeks to assign responsibility for fraudulent and unethical behaviour to an individual rather than inquiring as to the broader systems or culture that are likely to have been contributing factors.

Cases such as that of Jérôme Kerviel have led to reflection on whether one person can be held completely accountable for unethical behaviour given they operate in a broader system that can facilitate or 'turn a blind eye' to the actions of individuals. Kerviel was a trader for the French securities company Société Générale who lost more than US$7 billion in company assets by conducting a series of unauthorised and false trades between 2006 and early 2008. He was subsequently formally charged with abuse of confidence and illegal access to computers, and in 2010 he was sentenced to three years in prison for fraud and breach of trust and ordered to personally repay €4.9 billion. Throughout the public reporting of the case, Kerviel was characterised as a rogue trader; however, many have questioned how unauthorised trading of the magnitude involved could have gone unnoticed by other individuals and the systems that were designed to provide checks and safeguards. Kerviel claimed the practices in which he engaged were widespread and that making a profit made the hierarchy turn a blind eye. Interestingly, Kerviel is not thought to have personally profited from the trades.[11]

Dennis Gentilin was the individual publicly named as a whistleblower in the National Australia Bank foreign exchange trading scandal of 2004, which saw four traders jailed for unauthorised trading and cost the bank's CEO and chairman their jobs. He wrote in his 2016 book *The Origin of Ethical Failures: Lessons for Leaders*: 'As a starting point, any explanation of unethical behaviour must consider the environment within which the "bad apples" operate, recognising that it can have a profound effect on behaviour'. Gentilin continued: 'What's more, if an assessment of the environment reveals a rotten "barrel", then one will also find that the unethical behaviour is rarely constrained to a few "bad apples"—it has more than likely permeated the system'.[12]

In their paper 'The Normalization of Corruption in Organizations', Blake Ashforth of the W. P. Carey School of Business at Arizona State University, and Vikas Anand, professor of management at the University of Arkansas, identified socialisation as a factor in explaining how otherwise morally upright individuals can routinely engage in corrupt practices without experiencing conflict, and how corruption can persist despite the turnover of its initial practitioners. Importantly, they concluded that the individual as the 'evil-doer' misses the point that systems and individuals are mutually reinforcing.[13]

In 2010, John Hartman, a former employee of asset management company Orion, became the youngest person jailed for insider trading in Australia. The chief judge in the case, Peter McClellan, concluded when sentencing Hartman that the financial services industry had 'corrupted his values'.[14] Gentilin warned of this in his book when he said:

> As my experience in the FX trading scandal at the NAB taught me, young people in particular are vulnerable to embracing and endorsing immoral social norms. It is rare that a young person entering the workforce for the first time would have taken the time to seriously consider and explore their values and what is important to them.
>
> Having not calibrated their moral compass, young people are more likely to use environmental cues to help them determine what type of behaviour is appropriate. As [financial journalist] Michael Lewis rightly points out with reference to young people embarking on a career in finance, this can ultimately shape character.
>
> The question I've always had about this army of young people with seemingly endless career options who wind up in finance is: What happens next to them? People like to think they have a 'character', and that this character of theirs will endure, no matter the situation. It's not really so.
>
> People are vulnerable to the incentives of their environment, and often the best a person can do, if he wants to behave in a certain manner, is to choose carefully the environment that will go to work on his character.[15]

As calls for individual accountability in the finance sector continue, and regulations and sanctions are tightened to hold people to account, it is crucial that individuals remain aware of the influence of the environment on their decisions so they can moderate their behaviour accordingly. For some, it may result in a request to change teams or leaving an organisation, while others may utilise formal whistleblowing protections or raise issues through internal organisational mechanisms.

Regardless, it appears the individual will be held to account, if not by the formal regulatory and legal systems then by the sector itself. Notably, the path to professionalisation includes the ability of a profession to discipline individuals for not operating in accordance with agreed standards, its adherence to which it promotes to the public.

THE INFLUENCE OF OTHER PEOPLE

As with the influence of our environment, there also has been much research and academic commentary confirming the influence of other people on our decisions and behaviours. The bystander effect, or bystander apathy, is a phenomenon that was identified through social psychology and refers to cases in which individuals do not offer any means of help to a victim when other people are present. The probability of help is actually inversely related to the number of bystanders—in other words, the greater the number of bystanders, the less likely it is that any one of them will help someone in trouble.

A number of reasons have been identified to explain this, including ambiguity (doubts as to whether the victim really needs help), cohesiveness (groups with closer relationships being more likely to help) and diffusion of responsibility (believing someone else will take responsibility).[16] Robert Cialdini, regents' professor emeritus of psychology and marketing at Arizona State University, concluded in his 2008 book *Influence: Science and Practice* that when people are figuring out what to do in a new situation, they take their cue from what seems to be other people's normal behaviour. This is commonly referred to as the 'social norm'.[17]

Social researchers have also confirmed that the presence of others can lead people to behave more ethically, particularly if they know they're being watched. Studies have shown that even minimal cues that a person is being watched, such as a picture of eyes above an honour box at a communal coffee machine, can positively influence people's behaviour.[18]

The theory that human behaviour is determined by surrounding circumstances rather than by personal qualities is sometimes referred to as 'situationist', a term introduced by bioethics pioneer Joseph Fletcher.[19] According to situationist theory, our circumstances will largely drive our behaviour, and we may not be rational when it comes to our own moral behaviour.

The well-known 1971 Stanford prison experiment, conducted to study the psychological effects of ordinary people becoming a prisoner or prison guard, saw some participants through their roles as guards—influenced by authoritarian measures—ultimately subject some prisoners to torture, and many of the prisoners passively accept the abuse and obstruct others trying to stop it. The experiment vividly highlighted how situational forces can drive ordinary people to behave in ways that are not only totally out of character but also contrary to what most people would consider to be appropriate and ethical.[20]

Focus
Ethics Aside

At a 2014 responsible investment conference, a senior lawyer was called upon to provide her view on developments in fiduciary duties, focusing specifically on whether directors could exercise their decision-making to factor in such issues as climate change. When she commenced her talk with the words 'ethics aside', some were taken aback. Ethics is not just a field of philosophy but also a business practice, one the finance sector, for example, publicly champions and promotes internally.

Economists regularly engage in a similar rationalisation where they set aside a range of variable factors through the adoption of assumptions. Assumptions operate to simplify a discussion and allow for the setting of economic theories and models. Economics and the field of science tend to adopt a ceteris paribus approach, meaning 'other things equal'. This assumes that all other variables except those under immediate consideration are held to be constant.

Such practices might be considered necessary on a practical level, facilitating the adoption of frameworks and principles that can operate at the broadest level in the majority of situations. In turn, a clearer path for decision-making is established. However, if ethics is to be truly embedded across finance, and if the sector is to professionalise its people and practices, then ethics most certainly cannot be set aside. To do so risks descending into a rules-based culture where thinking, judgement and good decision-making are stifled. Assumptions and the ceteris paribus approach assist in creating a sense of certainty that does not always exist. If assumptions are accepted without question or review, then there is likely to be disappointment, perhaps even disbelief, in cases where exceptions are present.

The field of economics came into question following the 2007–08 global financial crisis, with economists called upon to defend their profession. In an *Atlantic* opinion piece in 2009, Richard Posner quoted prominent Harvard economist Greg Mankiw's defence of his field:

> It is fair to say that this crisis caught most economists flat-footed. In the eyes of some people, this forecasting failure is an indictment of the profession. But that is the wrong interpretation. In one way, the current downturn is typical: Most economic slumps take us by surprise. Fluctuations in economic activity are largely unpredictable. Yet this is no reason for embarrassment. Medical experts cannot forecast the emergence of diseases like swine flu and they can't even be certain what paths the diseases will then take. Some things are just hard to predict.

Posner goes on to say, 'Economists can't be blamed for having an imperfect understanding of depressions; these are immensely complex events. But they can be blamed for exaggerating their understanding of them'.[21]

Also in 2009, Sidney Winter, management professor at the Wharton School of the University of Pennsylvania, argued in an interview for the school's blog post that as computers have grown more powerful, academics have come to rely on mathematical models to figure out how various economic forces will interact. But many of these models simply dispense with certain variables that stand in the way of clear conclusions. Commonly missing are hard-to-measure factors like human psychology and people's expectations of the future.[22]

The reality is that ethical and moral considerations are part of our everyday lives, and the business community is no exception. Businesses are quite simply composed of individuals, and it is the values of those individuals that set the ethical tone and standards. To expect individuals to set aside their values and morals in the pursuit of work goals only serves to narrow their input and risk an isolation that is likely to be reflective of other stakeholders, such as customers.

The sustainability movement has forced a rethinking of the position of the economy as merely a subset of society, with society a subset of the environment.[23] This theory contrasts with the view of the economy as the central driving force of societal development. As the finance sector seeks to professionalise, the way in which it views both itself and the economy will be critical to changing behaviours and building and maintaining the trust of the community. The reality is that things aren't equal. Humans are not always predictable and there will be exceptions to rules. To deny this is to wilfully engage in a delusion.

Socrates claimed that 'the unexamined life is not worth living', a definitive and absolute statement. Dr Simon Longstaff, when reflecting on the uncompromising tone of Socrates' language in a 2013 piece for *NewPhilosopher*, said:

> As Socrates demonstrated in his own life and death, being fully human can be extremely challenging. In a world of abiding uncertainty and complexity one can recognise a certain attraction in not examining too much, for too long in life. Thus the allure of those who offer to provide clear answers, simple directions or precise instructions so that you may set aside examination and merely comply, or unthinkingly follow custom and practice—perhaps living a conventionally moral life rather than an examined ethical life. One can easily imagine how pleasant an unexamined life might be. And it is for this reason that I think Socrates makes his claim so uncompromising.[24]

Ethics should not be considered an optional extra to business or something that can be set aside. It may be helpful to consider ethics not as the garnish that enhances a meal but rather the plate on which the meal is served.

CONCLUSION

On reviewing the research and commentary on the potential influences on decision-making, including the environment, other people, biases and self-deception, it might be easy to conclude that humans are so flawed that it's surprising we can make good decisions at all. However, through developing an ethical awareness of these influences, and by practising good decision-making, individuals can develop as ethical professionals and leaders.

GOOD PRACTICES

There are good practices that can be adopted by individuals to ensure strong ethical work cultures and more ethical business outcomes. Regularly using a good decision-making model and incorporating simple integrity tests into everyday practices will result in a more thorough decision-making process that considers a range of stakeholder views and can be used to both explain and justify decisions.

GOOD DECISION-MAKING

The use of a good decision-making framework can assist in the development of ethical professionals. Through understanding the potential impact of decisions and exploring options to minimise harm and protect interests, positive outcomes for customers and the community can be maximised.

Good decision-making generally explores the question of 'What ought one to do?', as posed by Socrates. John Boatright, professor of business ethics at Loyola University Chicago, in his 2012 book *Ethics and the Conduct of Business*, wrote that 'some situations are easily handled because what ought one to do or what is right and wrong are evident. Those situations that give us pause or produce moral anguish require careful thought and ultimately an ability to engage in ethical reasoning'.[25]

Various decision-making frameworks and models are promoted by different organisations working to assist companies in embedding ethical practices and creating ethical work cultures. The models tend to share the common traits of developing a critical understanding, employing imagination, and self-reflection. Of course, decisions made in the context of business are often subject to additional pressures related to time, stress and, in some cases, professional isolation. A formal framework such as the one suggested below can assist individuals and teams in navigating their way to the most ethical outcome.

1. *Gathering and understanding:* This stage seeks to understand the dilemma through the gathering of facts and related information. One should ask, what exactly are we dealing with? Is it a matter of two bad options or choosing between a range of good options? Why is the path unclear? Have we got all the information? Are there non-negotiables? At this stage, it is important to distinguish between facts and assumptions.

2. *Considering the context:* This stage seeks to understand and account for the context within which the dilemma has presented. It will include an analysis of the business environment that addresses the broader societal context, and consideration of which ethical theory (as outlined in Chapter 1) might be at play. One should ask, what are the minimum legal requirements? Do we believe we are morally right given

the context? What is usually done? What is best practice, or are there new developments? Are there different views within the team? Are there biases at play? Are there professional and organisational codes that apply?

3. *Considering others:* This stage seeks to factor in the views and interests of a range of stakeholders. The first task is to list the stakeholders who may be impacted by the decision and determine their wants, interests and needs. It should then become clear where they compete. Tensions should be identified and discussion pursued as to how the different interests can be prioritised to achieve the best outcome for all.

    At this stage one should consider their own and team members' gut reactions by asking if individuals are strongly drawn to the view of a particular stakeholder over another. And if so, why? This stage is a good time to apply an ethical lens by considering in turn the ethical theories of utilitarianism, duties and rights, virtue and relativism (again, as outlined in Chapter 1).

4. *Thinking of options:* This stage seeks to generate a range of possible options through an open and non-judgemental process. One should ask, what are the options? Individuals should employ imagination to think outside any limits, engaging in brainstorming and even allowing for proposals that might seem ridiculous. The use of a variety of lenses or positions can be used to consider the dilemma; for example, looking for a solution from a utilitarian, duties and rights, relativist or virtue perspective.

5. *Deciding and testing:* This stage seeks to refine the ideas and test whether they are appropriate. As options are selected and tested, one should ask, what would others think? Can we defend our position? Teams could hold a trial press conference to determine if the position is robust enough to withstand scrutiny.

    This is the time to be the devil's advocate, where one argues against a cause or position for the sake of an argument. In the context of good decision-making, this will assist in determining the validity of the position before others do, publicly.

6. *Reflection:* This stage seeks to formally incorporate the important practice of reflection. Individuals and teams can ask the following questions: Did it go as planned? Is there feedback that changes the basis for the decision? Have markets changed? Have circumstances changed and new considerations now need to be incorporated? Does it still feel right? While it may seem that the pace of business does not always allow for extensive reflection, the practice can still be encouraged and even formalised as part of team meetings, business reporting and individual performance appraisals.

As Joseph DesJardins outlined in his 2011 text *An Introduction to Business Ethics*, the final and ongoing part of ethical decision-making is to monitor and learn from the results of a decision.[26] Similarly, Giada Di Stefano, Francesca Gino, Gary Pisano and Bradley Staats concluded in their paper 'Learning by Thinking: How Reflection Improves Performance' that reflection is the powerful mechanism behind learning,[27] confirming the words of American philosopher, psychologist and educational reformer John Dewey: 'We do not learn from experience ... we learn from reflecting on experience'.[28]

Also worth consideration is the comprehensive Good Decision-Making model promoted by the Sydney-based Ethics Centre, which includes a Good Decision Pathway to evaluate potential choices to resolve an ethical dilemma.[29] Potential courses of action are subject to 'ethical tests' that involve responding to the following to form a matrix:

- maximises benefit over harm
- develops and maintains good character
- would make a good universal rule
- protects fundamental moral rights
- you would support it in public
- promotes a common good for the purpose
- applies stated values and principles
- you could live with it if it were done to you
- promotes care for others and relationships.

TESTS OF INTEGRITY

Undoubtedly, the speed of business does not always allow for the comprehensive process required of a good decision-making framework, and there will be many decisions that must rely on experience and good judgement. Paul Robertson, former treasurer of Macquarie Bank, who also held the position of integrity officer with the organisation, has said that he promoted two simple tests to ensure ethical decision-making in such situations: the 'put yourself in the other person's shoes' test, and the 'front page of the newspaper test'.[30] In the context of Australia, Robertson called the latter 'the Fin Review test', an abbreviation for *The Australian Financial Review*, the Australian business and finance newspaper published by Fairfax Media—as it involves considering the threat of something becoming public, this is also known as a 'sunlight test'.

Of course, if these decisions cannot be answered in the affirmative, then time must be put aside for the use of a good decision-making framework.

Case Study
Ethical Leadership and Commissions

Commissions refer to a payment for services or products sold. These payments are generally calculated on a percentage basis and are a common way of rewarding salespeople. In financial services, commissions have been applied to the work of mortgage brokers, financial planners, and various superannuation and trading positions. There are upfront commissions, paid at the time a product is sold or at the time of investment, and also trailing commissions, which are paid on a periodic basis until the product or investment is withdrawn.

An alternative to commissions is a fee-for-service payment, and this practice is increasingly being adopted by companies, and in some cases legislated. Steve Tucker, former CEO of MLC, could be considered to have demonstrated ethical leadership when he implemented the fee-for-service approach at MLC in 2006. In accordance with the idea of professional standards, he said that 'an industry that self-regulates is important for a sustainable future'.[31] Tucker consciously used the language of ethics in explaining his decision-making as a leader of the sector. His commitment to self-regulation and high ethical standards was also demonstrated by his position as a founding director of The Banking and Finance Oath, the industry-led initiative designed to reassert the ethical foundation of finance.

Following the leadership of Steve Tucker, the banning of upfront and trailing commissions become law under the Australian Government's Future of Financial Advice reforms in 2013.

ETHICAL LEADERSHIP

As argued earlier, work cultures are important as they have a significant impact on decision-making, signalling what is right and wrong. All individuals in a work culture have the ability to contribute to it, for better or worse. That said, leaders and senior executives have a particular responsibility to shape their immediate work environment so that good decision-making practices are developed and consistently supported. Creating a corporate culture in which individuals are both empowered and expected to make ethically responsible decisions is a necessary part of being an ethical business leader.

Another important element of ethical leadership is defining the goal towards which one is leading others. Rather than focusing purely on productivity, efficiency or profitability, an ethical leader will consider, for example, diversity, a range of stakeholder views, and impact, in determining goals and measures of success for their team or division.

In addition, for individuals to believe in a leader, they must trust them, and this trust must be earned. Earning trust takes time and relies on a leader being open and honest. Trust can quickly disintegrate if suspicion arises about the motives of someone's actions.

Philippa Foster Back, director of the London Institute of Business Ethics, argued in her 2005 book *Setting the Tone: Ethical Business Leadership* that society needs trust because we have to be able to rely on others acting as they say they will, and because we need others to accept that we will act as we say we will.[32] Executives and leaders wishing to set the tone within their organisation soon realise that trust begins with them.

Greg Medcraft, chairman of the Australian Securities and Investments Commission, has talked publicly of the critical role of leadership in creating a trusted and ethical financial services sector. In April 2016, he said: 'If a customer trusts you, that's the foundation of a long-term business. So a crucial task for leaders is to whittle out whatever company characteristics lead to a lack of consumer trust—people, processes or products'. Medcraft also identified the trust of colleagues as being crucial: 'Good leadership is not just about passion or good technical skills ... Most of all you have to bring people with you'.[33]

In *Setting the Tone*, Philippa Foster Back identified five key attributes of an ethical leader:

1. openness
2. fair-minded
3. honesty
4. courage
5. the ability to listen.

These attributes set an ethical leader apart from other leaders. Individuals will possess these attributes in varying degrees; however, they will be nurtured, developed and supported in an ethical leader.

Leaders must also behave in a way that will encourage others to behave similarly. It is important that an ethical leader is:

- open-minded and cultivates themselves and others through a willingness to learn
- independent and willing to stand up and be counted, including challenging the status quo
- determined to act without fear of confrontation, actively addressing poor behaviour
- considerate in managing expectations
- aware that doing the right thing is the right thing to do.

Many leaders must also manage trust outside their organisation; for example, directly with customers and other stakeholders. This trust can be built up by openly and honestly explaining decisions and actions.

The ability to identify ethical dilemmas and deal with them appropriately is another important skill for leaders to develop. Ethical dilemmas commonly arise due to tensions between the wants and interests of different parties, and when the boundaries of right and wrong are not clear. Individuals can be faced with various options, including choices between two 'rights' or recognition of the 'least wrong'. According to John Boatright in the 2008 publication *Ethics in Finance*, some of the most difficult dilemmas of business life can occur when individuals become aware of questionable behaviour by others or are pressured to engage in it themselves. Wrongdoing can also occur in large organisations, where responsibility is diffused among many individuals and no one person is 'really' responsible.[34]

Rather than relying on instinct or experience, individuals can be guided by a combination of internal procedures and, importantly, good decision-making practices, as supported by the leadership of an organisation. It is important to recognise that there are leaders at every level of an organisation; for example, there are division leaders, team leaders and project leaders. There are also informal leaders, those who have no title at all yet have the respect and trust of others. Each leader will, by example, have an effect on other people and the environment.

While theories of leadership are constantly evolving, individuals should take some comfort from the fact that many of the attributes and behaviours of ethical leaders are common in people's nature, and developing them is merely a matter of becoming self-aware and finding an environment and people that can nurture individual ethical leadership capabilities.

CONCLUSION

Ethics should inform the everyday practices of individuals working in finance. Developing ethical awareness through understanding biases and considering competing interests will allow individuals to adjust their decisions and behaviours to achieve more-ethical outcomes. Ethical awareness also involves accounting for the influences of both the environment and other people. The use of a good decision-making model and the adoption of simple tests of integrity can ensure that processes are ethical, thorough, and will hold up to public scrutiny. All individuals should aspire to be ethical leaders. For a leader to be trusted, they must be trustworthy, and a commitment to ethical practices can ensure this is the case.

CONCLUSION
Get It Right the First Time

Banks are large, complex organisations with many stakeholders. These stakeholders are not just confined to customers and shareholders. Therefore, only looking after these two groups is no longer sufficient. We expect our banks to grow the economy sensibly, spread prosperity fairly, encourage entrepreneurship, improve financial literacy, help people overcome financial hardship, and be a responsible part of the community fabric.

These heightened community expectations are now being reflected in the banks' public communications. In the Commonwealth Bank of Australia's (CBA) 2016 annual report, chairman David Turner noted the ambition to secure and enhance the financial wellbeing of the bank's many stakeholders, broadly defined as *people, business and communities*. In achieving this, the bank committed itself to upholding integrity, accountability, collaboration, excellence and service. Specifically, Turner mentioned that in the previous three years, CBA had implemented programs that strengthened those values through behavioural expectations, embedded in the bank's culture.[1]

In 2016, almost 450 000 people were employed in the financial and insurance services sector in Australia. The four pillars of Australian banking collectively employed over 160 000 people in Australia and overseas. This vast workforce provides fundamental services that facilitate our daily lives, improve our living standards and support our prosperity into the future. In carrying out these services, few employees consider that any particular transaction can be perceived as ethically questionable. In fact, very few people set out to deliberately engage in ethical misconduct. Whether they are motivated by good intentions, solid principles or pursuit of the good life, most people want to be honest, act with integrity and be trusted. But work and circumstances occasionally intervene and people end up doing the wrong thing, knowingly or not. In some cases, their ethics are gradually eroded by a bad workplace culture; in others, a switch is flicked if a 'too good to be true' opportunity arises. All too often an individual may not even notice that they have crossed a line. What is fair, what is just, and how far fiduciary duty extends, may not be obvious.

The ethical issues raised in this book are not new. Getting governance right, prioritising duties to clients while recognising duties to employers and stakeholders, declaring and managing conflicts of interest, all have been textbook material for a long time. This suggests ongoing concerns about finance sector ethics. The deregulation of financial institutions and markets may well have invited unscrupulous behaviour in the pursuit of market share. Yet the benefits of competition and support of economic growth may be considered to outweigh the costs, even if not always. This is not to say that we should be complacent and just accept bad behaviour or unethical practices. Unless we continue to address ethical misconduct, then poor practices will become acceptable and we risk further eroding trust in this so vital of sectors.

Regulators need to get better at detecting, prosecuting and deterring unethical conduct, and of course they need to have the resources to do so. Legislators need to continue to close loopholes, and review penalties to ensure they are effective. But more than external pressure, the management and board members of our major financial institutions need to take responsibility and self-regulate their institutions and the sector.

The 2007–08 global financial crisis and the subsequent taxpayer-funded bailouts of the world's leading banks put those banks in the public spotlight. An era of exuberance and creative financial engineering would, it seemed, come to an end, to be replaced by moderation and a 'back to basics' service approach. However, many are still waiting for the evidence this has happened or is happening. Reading the chair statements of financial institutions in their annual reports suggests that the banks are attempting to again take ownership of this revised agenda.

But it's not the same old banking anymore. The digital revolution has unlocked the financial system in ways that threaten the dominance, and the sustainability, of the old financial establishment. Fintech could hold the key to improved trust in financial institutions, or contribute to its further undoing.

Internet banking and robot advice may appear to be free from human intervention; however, the ethics of the programming and underlying algorithms are already being questioned. Transparency and efficiency have been greatly enhanced by digital technology, yet new ethical dilemmas have also been created—the privacy and confidentiality of customer data; an inability to express compassion, support and, importantly, a truly human understanding of the all-important customer. These dilemmas are equally disadvantageous for customers as for the banking system from which we are evolving.

Fintech competes with traditional banks by providing financial services using low-cost digital platforms, effectively eliminating labour cost from standardised services. At the same time, these low-cost platforms, such as pop-up crowdfunding, provide financial market access to social entrepreneurs and others who may not otherwise have it. Better yet, they may allow the finance sector to finally address the persistent exclusion of the un(der)banked from basic financial services through microfinance and peer-to-peer banking services provided through niche fintech providers.

These exciting new initiatives may make finance look good to a sceptical public and offer hope to those who are distrustful of the large financial institutions. However, attempts by the fintech sector to label itself the ethical alternative—suggesting that traditional finance is almost by definition unethical—may not be enough to shift customers from traditional services. People are not yet leaving their financial providers in significant numbers, despite many of those providers attracting deep levels of distrust.

'Old' finance could certainly borrow from the financial entrepreneurs who espouse ethical values so passionately and convincingly. But only if those values take hold of corporate culture and are reflected in all products and services will the finance sector—old and new—have a chance at restoring its standing and holding that which is the most valuable: trust.

For the finance sector, it is, as it has always been, a matter of trust.

ACKNOWLEDGEMENTS

FROM PAUL KOFMAN

It has been a long journey from my first experience of investment banking as an intern at Pierson, Heldring & Pierson in Amsterdam to teaching and writing about ethics in finance. From the 1987 stock market crash to the brave new world of fintech, I have been intrigued by the transformative power of finance in facilitating economic activity, spreading economic prosperity and raising living standards. A life without finance would be all the poorer. I just want it to do even better.

Thank you to the University of Melbourne—the brightest students one could hope for, and the smartest academics, my colleagues in the finance department—for providing me with an ideal environment in which to experiment with new ways of engaging our students and enriching their studies with a deep understanding of why ethics matters. I am particularly grateful to Leila Mehrez, who provided research assistance, and to Carsten Murawski for many stimulating (and motivating) discussions on all matters finance.

I am truly grateful to the many dedicated finance professionals—bankers, advisers and regulators—who have taken the time to discuss and give their perspective on the issues we raise in *A Matter of Trust*.

A big thank you to my parents, who always reminded me to be honest, have integrity and tell the truth. Most importantly, they supported and encouraged me to seek my own path through education.

FROM CLARE PAYNE

Thank you to Paul Robertson, former treasurer of Macquarie Bank and now Chair of Social Ventures Australia, who first encouraged me onto the path of ethics in finance, and to Dr Simon Longstaff of The Ethics Centre, who has provided a constant sounding board and encouragement along the way which has helped keep the wind in my sails.

Thank you to Dr Bronwyn King for giving me a deep understanding of the impact of tobacco and for being so determined in asking the finance sector to prioritise tobacco-free investment in what we call 'the ultimate ethical case study' for finance.

Of course, I must acknowledge the leaders of the banking and finance sector who first met with me in 2005 to provide their thoughts on ethics, and to those who went on to join me in founding The Banking and Finance Oath (The BFO). The Signatories of The BFO give me faith that there are good people in finance working to do what is right.

And most importantly, thank you to my parents for providing me with the education and development to question and call out that which I don't think is right, even if it has meant a somewhat unique career path (and a little too much travel).

NOTES

INTRODUCTION

1 Shiller, Robert, *Finance and the Good Society*, Princeton University Press, Princeton, NJ, 2012.

2 Wells Fargo, *Wells Fargo & Company Annual Report 2002: One Strong Box*, 2002, http://www.wellsfargohistory.com/download/annualreports/2002annualreport_wf.pdf

1 MONEY FOR NOTHING—REPUTATION, TRUST AND ETHICS (BY PAUL KOFMAN)

1 Thomas, Landon, 'On Wall Street, a Rise in Dismissals over Ethics', *The New York Times – Business Day*, 29 March 2005.

2 Mintel, 'Treating Customers Fairly: What Is Fair in the Consumer's Eye?', 7 July 2006, http://marketresearchworld.net/content/view/767/48/

3 University of Chicago Booth School of Business and Kellogg, School of Management, Chicago Booth/Kellogg School Financial Trust Index, 2017, http://www.financialtrustindex.org/

4 Consumer Federation of America, '7th Annual Survey Suggests Erosion of Credit Score Knowledge', Press Release, 26 June 2017, http://consumerfed.org/press_release/7th-annual-survey-suggests-erosion-credit-score-knowledge/

5 Pileggi, Leteisha, 'Home Loan Innovation', Mortgage Choice, 6 July 2014, https://www.mortgagechoice.com.au/leteisha.pileggi1/blog/home-loan-innovation-31476

6 That is not to say that the health sector has a perfectly clean slate when it comes to abuse of knowledge.

7 Yeates, Clancy, 'Future Fund Says Finance Lacks Professionalism', *The Sydney Morning Herald*, 1 June 2016.

8 Insurance Council of Australia, *Too Long; Didn't Read: Enhancing General Insurance Disclosure*, October 2015, http://www.insurancecouncil.com.au/assets/Effective%20Disclosure%20Report.pdf

9   Meadows, Donella H, Dennis L Meadows, Jorgen Randers and
     William W Behrens III, *The Limits to Growth*, Universe Books,
     New York, 1972.

10   Lucas Jr, Robert E, 'On the Mechanics of Economic
     Development', *Journal of Monetary Economics*, vol. 22, no. 1,
     1988, pp. 3–42.

11   Levine, Ross, 'Financial Development and Economic Growth:
     Views and Agenda', *Journal of Economic Literature*, vol. 35,
     no. 2, 1997, pp. 688–726.

12   Cecchetti, Stephen G, and Enisse Kharroubi, 'Why Does Financial
     Sector Growth Crowd out Real Economic Growth?', Working
     Paper no. 490, Bank for International Settlements, February 2015.

13   Yeates, Clancy, 'How a Loss of Trust Hurts the Economy', *The
     Sydney Morning Herald*, 14 June 2016.

14   Frost, Richard, 'China's $9.3t Stockmarket Has Investors Nervous
     Again', *The Sydney Morning Herald*, 19 April 2017.

15   Reserve Bank of Australia, 'Submission to the Financial System
     Inquiry', Occasional Paper no. 14, 1996, p. 12.

16   Arons, Steven, 'Deutsche Bank Pays $9.5b US Settlement for
     "Contributing Directly" to the GFC', *The Washington Post*,
     18 January 2017.

17   Piketty, Thomas, *Capital in the Twenty-First Century*, Harvard
     University Press, Cambridge, MA, 2013.

18   Cournede, Boris, and Oliver Denk, 'Finance, Growth and
     Inequality', OECD Insights: Debate the Issues, 29 March 2016,
     http://oecdinsights.org/2016/03/29/finance-growth-and-inequality/

19   Demirguc-Kunt, Asli, Leora Klapper, Dorothe Singer and Peter
     van Oudheusden, 'The Global Findex Database 2014: Measuring
     Financial Inclusion around the World', Policy Research
     Working Paper no. 7255, World Bank Group, 15 April 2015,
     http://www.worldbank.org/en/news/press-release/2015/04/15/
     massive-drop-in-number-of-unbanked-says-new-report

20   Sainsbury, Michael, 'Fintech Gold in Asia's Unbanked',
     InnovationAus.com, 30 October 2015, http://www.innovationaus.
     com/2015/10/FinTech-gold-in-Asia-s-unbanked/

21   Rogers, Ian, 'Sixteen Per Cent of People on Banking Margins',
     BankingDay, 18 May 2011, https://www.bankingday.com/nl06_
     news_selected.php?selkey=11677

22 CCP Research Foundation, 'Welcome to the Conduct Costs
    Project', 2017, http://conductcosts.ccpresearchfoundation.com/

23 Ferguson, Adele, 'Financial Misconduct Costs a Fortune', *The
    Sydney Morning Herald*, 17 September 2016.

24 Butler, Ben, 'ASIC Alert: "Ralph Norris Has Spoken"', *The
    Australian*, 22 April 2017.

25 Premeaux, Shane R, 'The Current Link between Management
    Behavior and Ethical Philosophy', *Journal of Business Ethics*,
    vol. 51, no. 3, 2004, pp. 269–78.

26 Smith, Adam, W Strahan and T Cadell, *An Inquiry into the
    Nature and Causes of the Wealth of Nations*, W Strahan and
    T Cadell, London, 1776.

27 Rahman, Faisel, 'Alternatives to Payday Lending Need Banks'
    Support', *The Guardian*, 25 August 2010.

28 Bell, Alex, 'The Co-op Bank Won't Finance Irresponsible
    Gambling Firms and Pay Day Lenders', *Manchester Evening
    News*, 20 January 2015.

29 Kant, Immanuel, *Groundwork of the Metaphysics of Morals*,
    Harper and Row Publishers, New York, 1964 (1785).

30 Ross, William David, *The Right and the Good*, Clarendon Press,
    Oxford, 1930.

31 Rawls, John, *A Theory of Justice*, Harvard University Press,
    Cambridge, MA, 1971.

32 Nozick, Robert, *Anarchy, State, and Utopia*, Blackwell Publishers,
    Oxford, 1993.

33 Burns, Kevin, 'Ethics Will Win in the Long Run', *Red Deer
    Express* (Alberta), 25 November 2004.

34 Aristotle, *Nicomachean Ethics* (trans.), Hackett Publishing
    Company, Indianapolis, IN, 1999 (1568).

35 Smith, Adam, W Strahan and T Cadell, *An Inquiry into the
    Nature and Causes of the Wealth of Nations*, W Strahan and
    T Cadell, London, 1776.

36 Bentham, Jeremy, *An Introduction to the Principles of Morals and
    Legislation*, Clarendon Press, Oxford, 1780.

37 Mill, John Stuart, *On Liberty*, John W. Parker & Son, London,
    1869.

38 Lim, Alvin, 'Don't Forget Asian Roots, Business Leaders Urged',
    The Straits Times (Singapore), 29 June 2012.

2 BETTER DAYS—THE SOCIAL CONTRACT (BY CLARE PAYNE)

1   Interview conducted with the author, 2017.

2   The Community Word, 'What Do You Call a Group of Geckos?', 7 July 2011, http://thecommunityword.com/online/cwnotes/2011/07/07/what-do-you-call-a-group-of-geckos/

3   Australian Government, *The Financial System Inquiry: Final Report*, 2014, chapter 4, http://fsi.gov.au/publications/final-report/chapter-4/

4   The Treasury, 'Future of Financial Advice', Australian Government, 2017, https://futureofadvice.treasury.gov.au/Content/Content.aspx?doc=home.htm

5   Parliament of Australia, *Report: Inquiry into Proposals to Lift the Professional, Ethical and Education Standards in the Financial Services Industry*, 19 December 2014, http://www.aph.gov.au/Parliamentary_Business/Committees/Joint/Corporations_and_Financial_Services/Financial_Adviser_Qualifications/Report

6   Münchenberg, Steve, submission to *Inquiry into Proposals to Lift the Professional, Ethical and Education Standards in the Financial Services Industry*, Australian Bankers' Association, 7 May 2015, https://www.treasury.gov.au/~/media/Treasury/Consultations%20and%20Reviews/Consultations/2015/Lifting%20the%20standards%20in%20the%20financial%20services%20industry/Submissions/PDF/Australian%20Bankers%20Association.ashx

7   Brown, Robert MC, 'Professionalising Financial Planning: Are We There Yet?', Professional Planner, 24 January 2016, http://www.professionalplanner.com.au/featured-posts/2016/01/24/professionalising-financial-planning-are-we-there-yet-43145/

8   Friedman, Fulton, 'A Friednzan Doctrine', *The New York Times*, 13 September 1970, http://www.nytimes.com/1970/09/13/archives/a-friedman-doctrine-the-social-responsibility-of-business-is-to.html

9   Friedman, Milton, 'The Social Responsibility of Business Is to Increase Its Profits', *The New York Times Magazine*, 13 September 1970.

10   Makower, Joel, 'Milton Friedman and the Social Responsibility of
     Business', GreenBiz, 24 November 2006, https://www.greenbiz.
     com/news/2006/11/24/milton-friedman-and-social-responsibility-
     business

11   Carroll, Archie B, 'Corporate Social Responsibility: Evolution
     of a Definitional Construct', *Business & Society*, vol. 38, no. 3,
     September 1999, pp. 268–95, http://www.academia.edu/419517/
     Corporate_Social_Responsibility_Evolution_of_a_Definitional_
     Construct

12   Keys, Tracey, Thomas W Malnight and Kees van der Graaf,
     'Making the Most of Corporate Social Responsibility', McKinsey
     & Company, December 2009, http://www.mckinsey.com/global-
     themes/leadership/making-the-most-of-corporate-social-
     responsibility

13   Freeman, R Edward, *Strategic Management: A Stakeholder
     Approach*, Pitman Publishing, New York, 1984.

14   International Organization for Standardization, 'ISO 26000:
     Social Responsibility', 2017, http://www.iso.org/iso/home/
     standards/iso26000.htm

15   Macquarie Group Foundation, '2017 Annual Review', 2017,
     http://www.macquarie.com/au/about/community/about-the-
     foundation/

16   Citigroup, 'Corporate Citizenship: Citi Foundation', 2017,
     http://www.citigroup.com/citi/citizen/foundation/

17   Responsible Investment Association Australasia, 'ESG Research
     Australia: About Us', 2017, http://responsibleinvestment.org/
     esgra/

18   Principles for Responsible Investment, 'About the PRI', 2017,
     https://www.unpri.org/about

19   Responsible Investment Association Australasia, 'About Us',
     2017, http://responsibleinvestment.org/about-us/

20   Program on Corporate Governance, *Engagement Strategies*,
     Harvard Law School, 2014, https://pcg.law.harvard.edu/
     wp-content/uploads/2015/12/esg-excerpt.pdf

21   Interview conducted with the author, 2017.

22   World Health Organization, *Tobacco Industry Interference
     with Tobacco Council*, WHO Press, Geneva, 2008, p. 22,

http://www.who.int/tobacco/resources/publications/Tobacco%20
Industry%20Interference-FINAL.pdf

23 Ibid., p. v.

24 European Network for Smoking and Tobacco Prevention, 'Global
    Tobacco Investments: the Fight for Tobacco-free Pension Funds',
    2017, http://ensp.org/2017/03/03/global-tobacco-investments-the-
    fight-for-tobacco-free-pension-funds-and-more/

25 U.S. Federal Trade Commission (FTC), *Cigarette Report for 2012*,
    2015, https://www.ftc.gov/system/files/documents/reports/federal-
    trade-commission-cigarette-report-2012/150327-2012cigaretterpt.
    pdf; see also, FTC, *Smokeless Tobacco Report for 2012*, 2015,
    https://www.ftc.gov/system/files/documents/reports/federal-
    trade-commission-smokeless-tobacco-report-2012/150327-2012
    smokelesstobaccorpt.pdf (data for top five manufacturers only).

26 National Cancer Institute, 'The Role of the Media in Promoting
    and Reducing Tobacco Use, Smoking and Tobacco Control',
    Monograph no. 19, NIH Pub. no. 07-6242, June 2008, http://
    cancercontrol.cancer.gov/tcrb/monographs/19/m19_complete.pdf

27 Angus, K, et al., 'The Effect of Tobacco Control Mass Media
    Campaigns, Counter-Advertising, and Other Related Community
    Interventions on Youth Tobacco Use', University of Stirling,
    Institute for Social Marketing, January 2008; see also, Wakefield,
    M, et al., 'Youth Responses to Anti-Smoking Advertisements
    from Tobacco-Control Agencies, Tobacco Companies, and
    Pharmaceutical Companies', *Journal of Applied Social
    Psychology*, vol. 35, no. 9, 2005, pp. 1894–911; Henriksen,
    L, et al., 'Industry Sponsored Anti-smoking Ads and Adolescent
    Reactance: Test of a Boomerang Effect', *Tobacco Control*, vol. 15,
    2006, pp. 13–18.

28 Banks, E, et al., 'Tobacco Smoking and All-cause Mortality in a
    Large Australian Cohort Study: Findings from a Mature Epidemic
    with Current Low Smoking Prevalence', *BMC Medicine*, vol. 13,
    no. 38, 2015, pp. 1–10, http://www.biomedcentral.com/content/
    pdf/s12916-015-0281-z.pdf

29 Tobacco Unfiltered, 'Cigarette Butts Are Toxic Waste', 9 April
    2013, http://www.tobaccofreekids.org/tobacco_unfiltered/
    post/2013_04_09_legacy

30 World Health Organization, *The Global Tobacco Crisis*, 2008, http://www.who.int/tobacco/mpower/mpower_report_tobacco_crisis_2008.pdf

31 ABC News, 'Bill Gates, Michael Bloomberg Launch Anti-tobacco Industry Legal Fund', 19 March 2015, http://www.abc.net.au/news/2015-03-19/bill-gates-michael-bloomberg-launch-anti-tobacco-industry-fund/6331986

32 Morgan Stanley Institute for Sustainable Investing, *Sustainable Signals: The Individual Investor Perspective*, February 2015, https://www.morganstanley.com/sustainableinvesting/pdf/Sustainable_Signals.pdf

33 U.S. Trust, *Annual Survey of High-net-worth and Ultra-high-net-worth Americans*, 2016, http://www.ustrust.com/publish/content/application/pdf/GWMOL/USTp_ARXDJKR8_2017-05.pdf

34 Tobacco Free Portfolios, 2017, http://www.tobaccofreeportfolios.org/

35 AXA, 'AXA Group Divests Tobacco Industry Assets', Press Release, 23 May 2016, https://www.axa.com/en/newsroom/press-releases/axa-divests-tobacco-industry-assets

36 Impact Investing Australia, 'Case Studies: Australia', 2017, http://impactinvestingaustralia.com/case-studies-examples/

37 Porter, Michael E, and Mark R Kramer, 'Creating Shared Value', *Harvard Business Review*, January–February 2011, https://hbr.org/2011/01/the-big-idea-creating-shared-value

38 Shared Value Project, 'Resources: Case Studies', 2017, http://sharedvalue.org.au/resources/case-studies/

39 United Nations, 'UN, Private Sector to Create Platform for Financing SDGs', Sustainable Development Goals, 2016, http://www.un.org/sustainabledevelopment/blog/2016/10/un-private-sector-to-create-platform-for-financing-sdgs/

40 *Australian Financial Review*, 'Gillian Triggs Urges Super Funds to Take up the Fight on Human Rights', 10 May 2016, http://www.afr.com/news/policy/gillian-triggs-urges-super-funds-to-take-up-the-fight-on-human-rights-20160509-gopw7d#ixzz4VV8aSi8t

41 Egan, Matt, '5,300 Wells Fargo employees fired over 2 million phony accounts', CNN Money, 9 September 2016, http://money.cnn.com/2016/09/08/investing/wells-fargo-created-phony-accounts-bank-fees/

42 Wells Fargo, 'Our Values', 2017, https://www.wellsfargo.com/
    about/corporate/vision-and-values/our-values/

43 Lencioni, Patrick M, 'Make Your Values Mean Something',
    Harvard Business Review, July 2002, https://hbr.org/2002/07/
    make-your-values-mean-something

44 Ferguson, Adele, 'Can't', *The Sydney Morning Herald –
    Business Day*, 2016, http://www.smh.com.au/interactive/2016/
    comminsure-exposed/terminal-illness/

45 Australian Government, *Final Report: Performance of the
    Australian Securities and Investments Commission*, 26 June 2014,
    http://www.aph.gov.au/Parliamentary_Business/Committees/
    Senate/Economics/ASIC/Final_Report/index

46 Yeates, Clancy, 'CBA Wants to Be "the Ethical Bank"', *The
    Sydney Morning Herald*, 18 November 2015, http://www.smh.
    com.au/business/banking-and-finance/cba-wants-to-be-the-ethical-
    bank-20151117-gl11rc.html

47 Australian Prudential Regulation Authority, 'Risk Culture',
    Information Paper, October 2016, p. 17, http://www.apra.gov.
    au/CrossIndustry/Documents/161018-Information-Paper-Risk-
    Culture.pdf

48 Weaver, GR, LK Treviño and PL Cochran, 'Corporate Ethics
    Practices in the Mid-1990's: An Empirical Study of the Fortune
    1000', *Journal of Business Ethics*, vol. 18, no. 3, 1999, pp. 283–
    94, http://link.springer.com/article/10.1023/A:1005726901050

49 The Ethics Centre, 'Ethical Literacy Program Launched', 27
    July 2015, http://www.ethics.org.au/on-ethics/blog/july-2015/
    ethical-literacy-program-launched

50 Delaney, JT, and DJ Sockell, 'Do Company Ethics Training
    Programs Make a Difference? An Empirical Analysis', *Journal
    of Business Ethics*, vol. 11, no. 9, 1992, pp. 719–27, http://link.
    springer.com/article/10.1007%2FBF01686353

51 Gray, Joanne, 'NAB Chairman Ken Henry Says Boards Should
    Talk Often to All Staff, Not Just Executives', *Australian Financial
    Review*, 4 April 2016, http://www.afr.com/leadership/nab-
    chairman-ken-henry-says-boards-should-talk-often-to-all-staff-
    not-just-executives-20160403-gnx43e

52 The Ethics Centre, 'Five Virtues of Ethical Leadership
    According to ASIC's Greg Medcraft', 6 April 2016,

http://www.ethics.org.au/on-ethics/blog/april-2016/
five-virtues-of-ethical-leadership-according-to-as

53 Bank Governance Leadership Network, 'Addressing Conduct and
Culture Issues in Banking', *ViewPoints*, 28 April 2015, http://
www.ey.com/Publication/vwLUAssets/ey-long-term-challenge-in-
addressing-conduct-and-culture-in-banking/$FILE/ey-long-term-
challenge-in-addressing-conduct-and-culture-in-banking.pdf

54 EthicalSystems.org, 'Corporate Culture: Introduction', 2017,
http://ethicalsystems.org/content/corporate-culture

55 Whittaker, Noel, 'Banks Are to Blame for Public Backlash',
Courier Mail, 17 April 2016, p. 73.

56 Han, Misa, 'Large Trader Bonuses Breed Arrogance, Risky
Market Behaviour', *Australian Financial Review*, 20 January
2016, p. 8.

57 Boyd, Tony, 'Bank Salaries Are Ridiculous', *Australian Financial
Review*, 12 November 2015, p. 64.

58 PwC, *Time to Listen*, 2016, http://www.pwc.co.uk/services/
human-resource-services/insights/time-to-listen.html

59 Young, Harrison, '*Star Wars* and Risk Culture: the Parallels Are
Striking', *Australian Financial Review*, 6 April 2016, http://www.
afr.com/business/banking-and-finance/star-wars-and-risk-culture-
the-parallels-are-striking-20160405-gnyrfp

60 Productivity Commission, *Executive Remuneration in Australia*,
Productivity Commission Inquiry Report no. 49, 19 December
2009, http://www.pc.gov.au/inquiries/completed/executive-
remuneration/report/executive-remuneration-report.pdf

61 Carew, Edna, *Westpac: the Bank that Broke the Bank*, Doubleday,
Sydney, 1997.

62 Boyd, Tony, 'Bank Salaries Are Ridiculous', *Australian Financial
Review*, 12 November 2015, p. 64.

63 Cable, Dan, and Freek Vermeulen, 'Stop Paying Executives for
Performance', *Harvard Business Review*, 23 February 2016,
https://hbr.org/2016/02/stop-paying-executives-for-performance

64 Hodgson, Paul, 'Top CEOs Make More than Three Times
the Average Worker', *Fortune*, 22 June 2015, http://fortune.
com/2015/06/22/ceo-vs-worker-pay/

65 Gavett, Gretchen, 'CEOs Get Paid too Much, According to
Pretty Much Everyone in the World', *Harvard Business Review*,

23 September 2014, https://hbr.org/2014/09/ceos-get-paid-too-much-according-to-pretty-much-everyone-in-the-world

66 Moriarty, Jeffrey, 'Do CEOs Get Paid Too Much?', *Business Ethics Quarterly*, vol. 15, no. 2, April 2005, pp. 257–81.

67 PwC, *Time to Listen*, 2016, http://www.pwc.co.uk/services/human-resource-services/insights/time-to-listen.html

68 Ferguson, Adele, 'Survey Casts Light on Yawning "Trust Gap" for Banks', *The Sydney Morning Herald*, 24 September 2016, http://www.smh.com.au/business/comment-and-analysis/survey-casts-light-on-yawning-trust-gap-for-banks-20160923-grmyho.html

3 SOMETHING SO STRONG—FOUNDATIONS OF TRUST (BY CLARE PAYNE)

1 PYMNTS.com, 'Regulations, Regulators and the High Cost of Banking Compliance', 31 May 2016, http://www.pymnts.com/news/security-and-risk/2016/banks-spend-and-hire-in-new-regulatory-environment/

2 Australian Government, *The Financial System Inquiry: Interim Report*, 2014, chapter 7, http://fsi.gov.au/publications/final-report/chapter-4/http://fsi.gov.au/publications/interim-report/07-regulatory-architecture/regulatory-burden/

3 Hida, Edward, *Global Risk Management Survey*, 9th edition, Deloitte University Press, Westlake, TX, May 2015, https://dupress.deloitte.com/dup-us-en/topics/risk-management/global-risk-management-survey-financial-services.html

4 Lagarde, Christine, 'The Role of Personal Accountability in Reforming Culture and Behavior in the Financial Services Industry', speech on behalf of International Monetary Fund to New York Fed, 5 November 2015, https://www.imf.org/en/News/Articles/2015/09/28/04/53/sp110515

5 Alberici, Emma, 'Penalties Too Weak to Discourage Bankers' Bad Behaviour, ASIC Boss Greg Medcraft Says', ABC News, 19 October 2016, http://www.abc.net.au/news/2016-10-18/penalties-too-weak-to-discourage-banks-bad-behaviour:-asic-boss/7944570

6 Titcomb, James, 'The Banking Industry's Bill for Bad Behaviour: $300bn', *The Telegraph*, 13 November 2014,

http://www.telegraph.co.uk/finance/newsbysector/banksand
finance/11228773/The-banking-industrys-bill-for-bad-behaviour-
300bn.html

7 Lagarde, Christine, 'The Role of Personal Accountability in
Reforming Culture and Behavior in the Financial Services
Industry', speech on behalf of International Monetary Fund to
New York Fed, 5 November 2015, https://www.imf.org/en/News/
Articles/2015/09/28/04/53/sp110515

8 Organisation for Economic Co-Operation and Development,
OECD *Principles of Corporate Governance*, 2004,
http://www.oecd.org/corporate/ca/corporategovernanceprinciples/
31557724.pdf

9 Bank for International Settlements, 'Principles for Enhancing
Corporate Governance', October 2010, http://www.bis.org/publ/
bcbs176.htm

10 Laker, John F, 'Corporate Governance in Financial Institutions',
Australian Prudential Regulation Authority, 19 October 2005,
http://www.apra.gov.au/Speeches/Documents/Corporate-
governance-in-Financial-Institutions-2.pdf

11 Wong, Simon CW, 'Boards: When Practice Isn't Enough',
McKinsey & Company, June 2011, http://www.mckinsey.com/
global-themes/leadership/boards-when-best-practice-isnt-enough

12 Ernst & Young, 'The Critical Role of the Board in Effective Risk
Oversight', 2013, http://www.ey.com/Publication/vwLUAssets/
The-critical-role-of-the-board-in-effective-risk-oversight/$FILE/
The-critical-role-of-the-board-in-effective-risk-oversight.pdf

13 MinterEllison, 'Institutional Investment, Corporate Governance
and Climate Change: What Is a Trustee to do?', 27 January 2015,
http://www.minterellison.com/publications/articles/Institutional-
investment-corporate-governance-and-climate-change-what-is-a-
trustee-to-do/

14 Chartered Accountants ANZ, *A Question of Ethics: Navigating
Ethical Failure in the Banking and Financial Services Industry*,
future[inc], August 2016, p. 6.

15 Interview conducted with the author, 2017.

16 The Banking and Finance Oath, 'The Oath', 2017, http://www.
thebfo.org/The-Oath

4 THE TWIST—DUTIES (BY CLARE PAYNE)

1 CFA Institute, 'Code of Ethics and Standards of Professional Conduct', 2014, https://www.cfainstitute.org/Translations%20 of%20Code%20of%20Ethics%20and%20Standards%20 of%20Pr/english_code.pdf

2 Australian Securities & Investments Commission, 'Directors: What Are My Duties as a Director?', 2014, http://asic.gov. au/regulatory-resources/insolvency/insolvency-for-directors/ directors-what-are-my-duties-as-a-director/

3 *Story v NCSC* (1988) 13 NSWLR 661; 13 ACLR 225; 6 ACLC 560.

4 *R J Elrington Nominees Pty Ltd v Corporate Affairs Commission* (1989) 1 ACSR 93.

5 MinterEllison, 'Institutional Investment, Corporate Governance and Climate Change: What Is a Trustee to do?', 27 January 2015, http://www.minterellison.com/publications/articles/Institutional- investment-corporate-governance-and-climate-change-what-is-a- trustee-to-do/

6 Levy, Michelle, 'Unravelled: The Best Interests Duties – Process or Outcome?', Allens, 5 February 2015, http://www.allens.com.au/ pubs/fsr/150205-unravelled-02.htm

7 Freshfields Bruckhaus Deringer / UNEP FI Asset Management Working Group, *A Legal Framework for the Integration of Environmental, Social and Governance Issues into Institutional Investment*, UNEP FI, Geneva, 2005, p. 100.

8 For a comprehensive review of research on responsible investment performance, see: Asset Management Working Group of the UN Environment Programme Finance Initiative and Mercer, *Demystifying Responsible Investment Performance: A Review of Key Academic and Broker Research on ESG Factors*, October 2007, http://www.unepfi.org/fileadmin/documents/Demystifying_ Responsible_Investment_Performance_01.pdf

9 *ASIC v Hellicar* (2012) HCA 17.

10 *ASIC v Healey & Ors* (2011) FCA 717.

11 Levy, Michelle, 'Unravelled: The Best Interests Duties – Process or Outcome?', Allens, 5 February 2015, http://www.allens.com.au/ pubs/fsr/150205-unravelled-02.htm

12 Law Commission, *Fiduciary Duties of Investment Intermediaries*,
    2014, http://www.lawcom.gov.uk/project/fiduciary-duties-of-
    investment-intermediaries/

13 Principles for Responsible Investment, 'New Report Aims to End
    Debate about ESG and Fiduciary Duty', 7 September 2015,
    http://www.unpri.org/press/new-report-aims-to-end-debate-about-
    esg-and-fiduciary-duty/

14 Australian Psychological Society, 'Wellbeing at Work', 2017,
    https://www.psychology.org.au/psychologyweek/wellbeing-at-
    work/

15 Business in the Community, *Mental Health at Work Report
    2016*, http://wellbeing.bitc.org.uk/all-resources/research-articles/
    mental-health-work-report-2016

16 National Australia Bank, 'Our People: Health and Wellbeing',
    2017, http://www.nab.com.au/about-us/corporate-responsibility/
    our-people/health-and-wellbeing

17 Hunt, Vivian, Dennis Layton and Sara Prince, 'Why Diversity
    Matters', McKinsey & Company, January 2015, http://www.
    mckinsey.com/business-functions/organization/our-insights/
    why-diversity-matters

18 Australian Government Workplace Gender Equality Agency,
    'The Business Case for Gender Equality', March 2013, https://
    www.wgea.gov.au/sites/default/files/business_case_for_gender_
    equality.pdf

19 McDonald, P, and S Charlesworth, Prevention and Response in
    Workplace Sexual Harassment, 2012; unpublished manuscript
    which includes a summary of the relevant research.

20 Hewlett, Sylvia Ann, Melinda Marshall and Laura Sherbin, with
    Tara Gonsalves, *Innovation, Diversity and Market Growth*,
    Center for Talent Innovation, September 2013, http://www.
    talentinnovation.org/_private/assets/IDMG-ExecSummFINAL-
    CTI.pdf

21 Deloitte and Victorian Equal Opportunity & Human Rights
    Commission, *Waiter, Is that Inclusion in My Soup? A New Recipe
    to Improve Business Performance*, May 2013, https://www2.
    deloitte.com/content/dam/Deloitte/au/Documents/human-capital/
    deloitte-au-hc-diversity-inclusion-soup-0513.pdf

22 CFA Institute Research Foundation, *Gender Diversity in Investment Management*, 2016, https://d21wiec48mugw8. cloudfront.net/wp-content/uploads/2016/11/10164244/gender_ diversity_report.pdf

23 Women in Banking and Finance and the Australian Financial Markets Association, *Initiatives for Attracting Women into Banking and Finance in Australia*, 2016, http://www.afma.com.au/ afmawr/_assets/main/lib90021/initiatives%20for%20attracting%20 women%20into%20banking%20and%20finance.pdf

24 Commonwealth Bank of Australia, 'Diversity in Leadership', 2017, https://www.commbank.com.au/about-us/who-we-are/ opportunity-initiatives/opportunity-from-good-business-practice/ our-approach-to-diversity/diversity-in-leadership.html

25 Ernst & Young, 'Placing Gender on the Financial Services Agenda', 2016, http://www.ey.com/gl/en/industries/financial-services/ey-placing-gender-on-the-financial-services-agenda

26 Cut+Paste, 'CFA Advocates for Diversity in Financial Services with Launch of New Gender Study', Professional Planner, 10 November 2016, http://www.professionalplanner.com.au/ cut-and-paste/2016/11/10/cfa-advocates-for-diversity-in-financial-services-with-launch-of-new-gender-study-51297/

27 Brands, Raina, 'Killing the Competition', London Business School, 15 July 2014, https://www.london.edu/faculty-and-research/lbsr/killing-the-competition#.V2IQM5N97rk

28 Workplace Gender Equality Agency, *Gender Equity Insights 2016*, https://www.wgea.gov.au/sites/default/files/BCEC_WGEA_ Gender_Pay_Equity_Insights_2016_Report.pdf

29 Australian Bureau of Statistics, 'Average Weekly Earnings, May 2015', cat. no. 6302.0, Canberra.

30 Workplace Gender Equality Agency, 'Gender Pay Gap Statistics', September 2015.

31 DiTomaso, Nancy, 'Racism and Discrimination Versus Advantage and Favoritism: Bias for Versus Bias Against', *Research in Organizational Behavior*, vol. 35, 2015, pp. 57–77.

32 Bassett-Jones, Nigel, 'The Paradox of Diversity Management, Creativity and Innovation', *Creativity and Innovation Management*, vol. 14, no. 2, 2005, pp. 169–75.

33 Australian Bureau of Statistics, 'Reflecting a Nation: Stories from the 2011 Census', cat. no. 2071.0, Canberra.

34 Diversity Council Australia, *Capitalising on Culture: A National Survey of Australian Business Leaders*, 2013, https://www.dca. org.au/research/project/capitalising-culture

35 Barry, Bruce, and Thomas S Bateman, 'A Social Trap Analysis of the Management of Diversity', *The Academy of Management Review*, vol. 21, no. 3, 1996, pp. 757–90.

36 Rantall, Mark, 'Trust Is the Foundation of My Profession', The Banking and Finance Oath, 1 August 2014, http://www.thebfo. org/Blog/August-2014/Trust-is-the-foundation-of-my-profession

37 MacKenzie, RN, 'Language, Self and Business Ethics', *Journal of Markets and Morality*, vol. 3, no. 1, 2000.

5   INTO TEMPTATION—CONFLICTS OF INTEREST (BY PAUL KOFMAN)

1 Smith, Adam, W Strahan and T Cadell, *An Inquiry into the Nature and Causes of the Wealth of Nations*, W Strahan and T Cadell, London, 1776.

2 Investcorp, 'Alignment of Interests', 2017, http://www.investcorp. com/site/page/alignment-of-interests

3 Dunn, James, 'Investments that Will Grow', *The Australian*, 15 June 2011.

4 Legal Practitioners' Liability Committee, 'Client Consent Is Not a Cure for Conflict Ills', 7 November 2014, https://lplc.com.au/ blog/client-consent-cure-conflict-ills/

5 Law Offices of Stimmel, Stimmel, & Smith, 'The Fiduciary Duty: What Is It and What Does It Impose upon You?', 2017, http:// www.stimmel-law.com/en/articles/fiduciary-duty-what-it- and-what-does-it-impose-upon-you

6 Commonwealth Director of Public Prosecutions, 'Case Reports: Lukas Kamay and Christopher Hill', 2015, https://www.cdpp.gov. au/case-reports/lukas-kamay-and-christopher-hill

7 Riewe, Julie, 'Conflicts, Conflicts Everywhere: Remarks to the IA Watch 17th Annual IA Compliance Conference: The Full 360 View', U.S. Securities and Exchange Commission, 26 February 2015, http://www.sec.gov/news/speech/conflicts-everywhere-full- 360-view.html

8   Mercola, J, 'Collusion between Pharmaceutical Industry and Government Deepens', 2 August 2012, http://articles.mercola.com/sites/articles/archive/2012/08/02/merck-flu-vaccine-conflicts.aspx

9   Jensen, Michael C, and William H Meckling, 'Theory of the Firm: Managerial Behavior, Agency Costs and Ownership Structure', *Journal of Financial Economics*, vol. 3, no. 4, October 1976, pp. 305–60.

10   Productivity Commission, *Executive Remuneration in Australia*, Productivity Commission Inquiry Report no. 49, 19 December 2009, http://www.pc.gov.au/inquiries/completed/executive-remuneration/report/executive-remuneration-report.pdf

11   Balnaves-James, Aidan, 'The Ethics of Executive Compensation: A Matter of Duty', Seven Pillars Institute for Global Finance & Ethics, 15 June 2015, http://sevenpillarsinstitute.org/case-studies/the-ethics-of-executive-compensation-a-matter-of-duty

12   Productivity Commission, *Executive Remuneration in Australia*, Productivity Commission Inquiry Report no. 49, 19 December 2009, http://www.pc.gov.au/inquiries/completed/executive-remuneration/report/executive-remuneration-report.pdf

13   Erman, Michael, and Jessica Dye, 'Goldman Loses $20 Million Fee in Conflict of Interest Case', Reuters, 10 September 2012, http://www.reuters.com/article/us-goldman-kindermorgan-idUSBRE8891CW20120911

14   Moullakis, Joyce, 'Investment Banks' Culture of Conflict', *Australian Financial Review*, 16 December 2011, http://www.afr.com/it-pro/investment-banks-culture-of-conflict-20120415-j607r#ixzz4hPFARl3u

15   International Organization of Securities Commissions, *Report on Analyst Conflict of Interest*, September 2003, http://www.iosco.org/library/pubdocs/pdf/IOSCOPD152.pdf

16   Stewart, Tim, 'UBS Escapes Punishment over "Poles and Wires" Research', InvestorDaily, 23 December 2015, http://www.investordaily.com.au/regulation/38699-ubs-escapes-punishment-over-poles-and-wires-research

17   ASIC released its report on research analyst independence in 2003: Australian Securities & Investments Commission,

Research Analyst Independence, Report no. 24, August 2003, http://download.asic.gov.au/media/1310533/Analyst_Independence_Report.pdf; an updated report reviewing sell-side analyst confidentiality and conflicts of interest appeared in 2016: Australian Securities & Investments Commission, *Sell-side Research and Corporate Advisory: Confidential Information and Conflicts*, Report no. 486, August 2016, http://download.asic.gov.au/media/4213635/rep486-published-9-august-2016.pdf

18 Corwin, Shane, Stephannie Larocque and Mike Stegemoller, 'Investment Banking Relationships and Analyst Affiliation Bias: The Impact of the Global Settlement on Sanctioned and Non-Sanctioned Banks', *Journal of Financial Economics*, vol. 124, no. 3, 2017, pp. 614–31.

19 Retkwa, Rosalyn, 'Amid the Crisis, New Opportunities for Independent Research Analysts', *Institutional Investor* magazine, 26 October 2009.

20 European Securities and Markets Authority, 'Policy Activities: MIFID (II) and MIFIR', 2017, https://www.esma.europa.eu/policy-rules/mifid-ii-and-mifir

21 *The Economist*, 'Regulating Equity Research: Analysts Beware', 16 May 2014, http://www.economist.com/blogs/schumpeter/2014/05/regulating-equity-research

22 Gilpin, Kenneth N, '17 Cited in Insider Trading', *The New York Times*, 10 February 1995, http://www.nytimes.com/1995/02/10/business/17-cited-in-insider-trading.html

23 English, Simon, 'Top Banker Faces £3m Insider Trading Charge', *The Independent*, 1 October 2012, http://www.independent.co.uk/news/business/news/top-banker-faces-3m-insider-trading-charge-8193214.html

24 Berkman, Henk, Paul D Koch and Joakim Westerholm, 'Personal Trading by Employees of Financial Intermediaries', Working Paper, November 2015, http://docplayer.net/10496025-Personal-trading-by-employees-of-financial-intermediaries.html

25 U.S. Securities and Exchange Commission, 'SEC Charges Hedge Fund Manager Leon Cooperman with Insider Trading', Press Release, 21 September 2016, https://www.sec.gov/news/pressrelease/2016-189.html

26 Commodity Futures Trading Commission, 'CFTC Files and Settles Action against Sumitomo Corporation for Manipulating the Copper Market in 1995–96', Press Release, 11 May 1998, http://www.cftc.gov/opa/enf98/opa4144-98.htm

27 Pender, Kathleen, 'Fake News Moves Markets But It's Nothing New', *San Francisco Chronicle*, 17 July 2015.

28 Gara, Antoine, 'Deutsche Bank Pays $2.5 Billion to Settle LIBOR Manipulation Suit', Forbes, 23 April 2015, https://www.forbes.com/sites/antoinegara/2015/04/23/deutsche-bank-pays-2-5-billion-to-settle-libor-manipulation-suit/#29b84595630d

29 Vaughan, Liam, Gavin Finch and Ambereen Choudhury, 'Traders Said to Rig Currency Rates to Profit Off Clients', Bloomberg, 11 June 2013, https://www.bloomberg.com/news/articles/2013-06-11/traders-said-to-rig-currency-rates-to-profit-off-clients

30 Australian Securities & Investments Commission, *Review of Financial Advice Industry Practice*, Report no. 251, 13 September 2011, http://download.asic.gov.au/media/1343702/rep251-published-13-September-2011.pdf

31 Yeates, Clancy, 'ASIC Wants Powers to Change High-risk Pay Structures', *The Age*, 27 April 2017.

32 The Treasury, 'Future of Financial Advice', Australian Government, 2017, https://futureofadvice.treasury.gov.au/Content/Content.aspx?doc=home.htm

33 Rose, Sally, 'Why Findex Boss Is Scrapping Commissions', *Australian Financial Review*, 22 July 2015.

34 Berenson, Alex, 'Enron's Collapse: the Rating Agencies; Debt Rankings Finally Fizzle, but the Deal Fizzled First', *The New York Times*, 29 November 2001, http://www.nytimes.com/2001/11/29/business/enron-s-collapse-rating-agencies-debt-rankings-finally-fizzle-but-deal-fizzled.html

35 Baghai, Ramin, and Bo Becker, 'Non-Rating Revenue and Conflicts of Interest', Swedish House of Finance, Research Paper no. 15-06, 16 November 2016, https://ssrn.com/abstract=2589519

36 Cecchetti, Stephen G, and Kermit L Schoenholtz, 'Credit Ratings and Conflicts of Interest', Money and Banking, 6 June 2016, http://www.moneyandbanking.com/commentary/2016/6/6/credit-ratings-and-conflicts-of-interest

37 Norris, Floyd, 'Moody's Official Concedes Failure in Some Ratings', *The New York Times*, 26 January 2008.

38 Dunckley, Mathew, 'No Conflict Problem Here, Says Hartzer', *The Age*, 9 May 2017.

39 Loewenstein, George, Daylian M Cain and Sunita Sah, 'The Limits of Transparency: Pitfalls and Potential of Disclosing Conflicts of Interest', *The American Economic Review*, vol. 101, no. 3, 2011, pp. 423–8.

40 Insurance Council of Australia, *Too Long; Didn't Read: Enhancing General Insurance Disclosure*, October 2015, http://www.insurancecouncil.com.au/assets/Effective%20Disclosure%20Report.pdf

41 Glassman, Cynthia, 'Speech by SEC Commissioner: Remarks before the Security Traders Association', U.S. Securities and Exchange Commission, 16 October 2003, http://www.sec.gov/news/speech/spch101603cag.htm

42 Cooper, Jeremy, 'Managing Conflicts of Interest in the Australian Financial Services Industry', Australian Securities and Investments Commission, Paper presented to Securities and Derivatives Industry Association Conference, 26 May 2006, http://download.asic.gov.au/media/2103226/managing_conflicts_of_interest.pdf

43 Commonwealth Bank of Australia, 'Policy for Managing Conflicts of Interest', 2017, https://www.commbank.com.au/corporate/research/conflicts-of-interest-policy.html

6 ONE STEP AHEAD—EVOLVING CHALLENGES (BY PAUL KOFMAN)

1 Bennet, Michael, 'Banks Feel the Heat as Small Enterprises Turn to Fintech Lenders', *The Australian*, 21 November 2015, http://www.theaustralian.com.au/business/financial-services/banks-feel-heat-as-small-business-turns-to-fintech-lenders/news-story/10b67fa5cce1d0ad2d61d8bbf0075904

2 Wall, Larry D, 'Two Drivers of Financial Innovation', Center for Financial Innovation and Stability, Federal Reserve Bank of Atlanta, February 2014, https://www.frbatlanta.org/cenfis/publications/notesfromthevault/1402

3   Ellerm, Jessica, 'The Ethical Conundrum at the Heart of Fintech and Banking', BankNXT, 14 March 2016, http://banknxt. com/56100/ethical-conundrum-fintech-banking/

4   Skinner, Chris, 'Hong Kong's Fintech Strategy', BankNXT, 11 May 2017, http://banknxt.com/60722/hong-kong-fintech-strategy/

5   Wolf, Martin, 'Good News: Fintech Could Disrupt Finance', *Financial Times*, 9 March 2016, https://www.ft.com/ content/425cb3ca-e480-11e5-a09b-1f8b0d268c39

6   KPMG International, *Making Hong Kong a FinTech Centre: Innovating Business in Asia*, June 2015, https://assets.kpmg. com/content/dam/kpmg/pdf/2015/06/Making-HK-FinTech-Centre-201506.pdf

7   Halverson, Mark, 'Big Data, Ethics, and Financial Services Firms' Moral Responsibility', *Digitalist Magazine*, 7 November 2013, http://www.digitalistmag.com/industries/insurance/2013/11/07/ big-data-ethics-financial-services-firms-moral-responsibility-video-0813684

8   Ethical Consumer, 'Buzz around Crowdfunding', March 2014, http://www.ethicalconsumer.org/ethicalreports/ethical-finance/ ethicalinvestments/introductiontocrowdfunding.aspx

9   Yeates, Clancy, 'Retail Investors Shift $45m from Banks into Peer to Peer Loans, *The Age*, 7 December 2016.

10   Todd, Sarah, 'Wells Fargo Bans Staff from Investing in P2P Loans', *Financial Times*, 21 January 2014, https://www.ft.com/ content/f3135594-7f82-11e3-b6a7-00144feabdc0

11   Salisbury, Ian, 'Lending Club's CEO Has Left and Its Stock Has Plunged: Should Lenders Bail Out?', Time.com – Money, 13 June 2016, http://time.com/money/4340588/peer-to-peer-lending-club-woes/

12   World Economic Forum, *The Role of Financial Services in Society: Understanding the Impact of Technology-enabled Innovation on Financial Stability*, 2016, http://www3.weforum. org/docs/WEF_FS_RoleFinancialServicesSociety_Stability_Tech_ Recommendations_2016.pdf

13   Banks are private institutions. Their significant role in society has given them a social licence to operate. The public would therefore consider banks to be semi-public institutions. Post bailouts, some banks did (at least temporarily) become actual public institutions.

14 Wildau, Gabriel, 'China Launches Fresh Attack on Shadow
    Banking Risk', *Financial Times*, 22 February 2017, https://www.
    ft.com/content/a7341efe-f8e4-11e6-9516-2d969e0d3b65

15 Elliott, Douglas J, Arthur R Kroeber and Yu Qiao, 'Shadow
    Banking in China: A Primer', The Brookings Institution, Economic
    Studies, March 2015, https://www.brookings.edu/wp-content/
    uploads/2016/06/shadow_banking_china_elliott_kroeber_yu.pdf

16 Tan, Su-Lin, 'Shadow Banks Surge amid APRA Crackdown',
    Australian Financial Review, 27 April 2017, http://www.afr.com/
    real-estate/shadow-banks-surge-amid-apra-crackdown-20170406-
    gvfeug

17 Associated Press, 'Hundreds of Suicides in India Linked to
    Microfinance Organizations', 25 February 2012.

7 TAKE THE PRESSURE DOWN—ETHICS INFORMING PRACTICE (BY CLARE PAYNE)

1 Kahneman, D, and G Klein, 'Strategic Decisions: When Can You
   Trust Your Gut?', *McKinsey Quarterly*, March 2010.

2 Smith, Adam, *The Theory of Moral Sentiments*, London and
   Edinburgh, 1759.

3 Smith, Adam, W Strahan and T Cadell, *An Inquiry into the
   Nature and Causes of the Wealth of Nations*, W Strahan and
   T Cadell, London, 1776.

4 Whitbourn, Michaela, 'Oliver Curtis, Husband of Roxy Jacenko,
   Jailed for Insider Trading', *The Sydney Morning Herald*, 24 June
   2016, http://www.smh.com.au/nsw/oliver-curtis-husband-of-roxy-
   jacenko-jailed-for-insider-trading-20160623-gpputd.html

5 Stout, Lynn, *Cultivating Conscience: How Good Laws Make
   Good People*, Princeton University Press, Princeton, NJ, http://
   press.princeton.edu/titles/9272.html

6 Knapp, John, *Self-deception and Moral Blindness in the Modern
   Corporation*, University of Wales, Lampeter, 1999.

7 Office of Diversity and Outreach, 'Unconscious Bias', University
   of California, San Francisco, 2017, https://diversity.ucsf.edu/
   resources/unconscious-bias

8 Dore, RA, KM Hoffman, AS Lillard and S Trawalter, 'Children's
   Racial Bias in Perceptions of Others' Pain', *British Journal of
   Developmental Psychology*, vol. 32, 2014, pp. 218–31.

9   Dasgupta, N, 'Implicit Attitudes and Beliefs Adapt to Situations: a Decade of Research on the Malleability of Implicit Prejudice, Stereotypes, and the Self-Concept', *Advances in Experimental Social Psychology*, vol. 47, 2013, pp. 233–79.

10 Salancik, Gerald, and Jeffrey Pfeffer, *The External Control of Organizations: a Resource Dependence Perspective*, Harper & Row, New York, 1978, https://www.gsb.stanford.edu/faculty-research/books/external-control-organizations-resource-dependence-perspective

11 Aldrick, Philip, 'Rogue Trader Jerome Kerviel Blames SocGen for €4.9bn Loss', *The Telegraph*, 4 June 2012, http://www.telegraph.co.uk/finance/financial-crime/9310909/Rogue-trader-Jerome-Kerviel-blames-SocGen-for-4.9bn-loss.html

12 Gentilin, D, *The Origins of Ethical Failures: Lessons for Leaders*, Routledge, Abingdon, UK, 2016.

13 Ashforth, Blake, and Vikas Anand, 'The Normalization of Corruption in Organizations', *Research in Organizational Behavior*, vol. 25, 2003, pp. 1–52.

14 Snow, Deborah, and Colin Kruger, 'Storm Clouds Gather for Society Banker', *The Sydney Morning Herald*, 2 February 2013, http://newsstore.fairfax.com.au/apps/viewDocument.ac;jsessionid=75E92919235CBD5ED2828080F7774066?sy=afr&pb=all_ffx&dt=selectRange&dr=1month&so=relevance&sf=text&sf=headline&rc=10&rm=200&sp=brs&cls=4343&clsPage=1&docID=SMH1302021J4F93FPNBF

15 Gentilin, D, *The Origins of Ethical Failures: Lessons for Leaders*, Routledge, Abingdon, UK, 2016.

16 Psychology Today, 'What Is the Bystander Effect?', 2017, https://www.psychologytoday.com/basics/bystander-effect

17 Cialdini, Robert B, *Influence: Science and Practice*, 5th edition, Allyn and Bacon, Boston, 2008.

18 MacKenzie, Debora, 'Big Brother' Eyes Make Us Act More Honestly', *New Scientist*, 28 June 2006, https://www.newscientist.com/article/dn9424-big-brother-eyes-make-us-act-more-honestly/

19 Fletcher, Joseph, *Situation Ethics: the New Morality*, Westminster Press, Philadelphia, 1966.

20 The Stanford Prison Experiment, 2017, http://www.prisonexp.org/

21 Posner, Richard A, 'An Economist Tries to Defend His
    Profession – and Fails', *The Atlantic*, 24 May 2009,
    http://www.theatlantic.com/business/archive/2009/05/
    an-economist-tries-to-defend-his-profession-and-fails/18191/

22 Wharton University of Pennsylvania, 'Why Economists
    Failed to Predict the Financial Crisis', Knowledge@Wharton,
    13 May 2009, http://knowledge.wharton.upenn.edu/article/
    why-economists-failed-to-predict-the-financial-crisis/

23 Reddy, TL, and RJ Thomson, 'Environmental, Social and
    Economic Sustainability: Implications for Actuarial Science',
    Presentation to Actuaries Institute 2015 ASTIN, AFIR/ERM
    and IACA Colloquia, August 2015, http://www.actuaries.
    asn.au/Library/Events/ASTINAFIRERMColloquium/2015/
    ReddyThompsonActuarialSciencePaper.pdf

24 Longstaff, Simon, 'The Unexamined Life Is Not Worth Living',
    NewPhilosopher, 2 June 2013, http://www.newphilosopher.com/
    articles/being-fully-human/

25 Boatright, JR, *Ethics and the Conduct of Business*, 7th edition,
    Pearson, Boston, 2012.

26 DesJardins, J, *An Introduction to Business Ethics*, 4th edition,
    McGraw-Hill, New York, 2011.

27 Di Stefano, G, F Gino, G Pisano and B Staats, 'Learning by
    Thinking: How Reflection Improves Performance', Working
    Knowledge, Harvard Business School, 11 April 2014, http://
    hbswk.hbs.edu/item/learning-by-thinking-how-reflection-
    improves-performance

28 Di Stefano, G, F Gino, G Pisano and B Staats, 'Making
    Experience Count: the Role of Reflection in Individual Learning',
    Harvard Business School, Working Paper no. 14-093, 5 December
    2016, http://papers.ssrn.com/sol3/papers.cfm?abstract_id=
    2414478

29 The Ethics Centre (previously known as St James Ethics Centre) is
    an independent, not-for-profit organisation that has been working
    for over twenty-five years to help people navigate the complexity
    and uncertainty of difficult ethical issues. It delivers innovative
    programs, services and experiences that are designed to bring ethics
    to the centre of professional and personal life, and align actions

with values and principles. More information and contact details can be found at the centre's website (http://www.ethics.org.au).

30 Interview conducted with the author, 2017.

31 Ibid.

32 Foster Back, Phillipa, *Setting the Tone: Ethical Business Leadership*, Institute of Business Ethics, London, 2005.

33 The Ethics Centre, 'Five Virtues of Ethical Leadership According to ASIC's Greg Medcraft', 6 April 2016, http://www.ethics.org.au/on-ethics/blog/april-2016/five-virtues-of-ethical-leadership-according-to-as

34 Boatright, JR, *Ethics in Finance*, 2nd edition, Blackwell Publishing, Malden, MA, 2008.

CONCLUSION: GET IT RIGHT THE FIRST TIME

1 Commonwealth Bank of Australia, *Annual Report 2016*, 2016, p. 4, https://www.commbank.com.au/content/dam/commbank/about-us/shareholders/pdfs/annual-reports/2016_Annual_Report_to_Shareholders_15_August_2016.pdf

INDEX